The Lost Art of Femininity

By Ayal Elbaz

ISBN: 978-83-955831-0-0

Table of Contents

Foreword

I began to feel intrigued by femininity, love, togetherness, romanticism and the opposite sex at a very young age. Essentially, as a boy, femininity was the thing that most drew me close to girls; it was a natural and very basic lure for me. Being a boy, I spent most of my time with other boys, but still I invested a considerable amount of time and effort looking for the company of girls, to be a part of their worlds. Principally, it seemed normal and natural to me that girls are the ones who should be pursued and courted, and the endeavour to have my world intertwine with theirs has forever been part of my life. Thus trying to get their attention and affinity was always a thing of importance for me growing up. I believe that an inner knowingness that men and women are supposed to be together, complement one another and create a strong and long-lasting emotional bond between them was ever present with me. And falling in love, wow, what a heart-warming feeling! What a beautiful mixture of emotions; excitement, longing, uncertainty, desire, apprehension and hope all bundled up together rendering one helpless, hopeless, happy and dreamful at the same time.

When I grew older, the feelings remained the same but were then more focused on the one girl rather than a general thing. But persistently and without alteration I have been feeling that fascination with and admiration of femininity. It has been a quality that has never failed to have an impact on me – similar to a beautiful song, a gorgeous oil painting or an exquisite landscape, except none of the above contained the most important quality of them all – life – whereas women did.

Alas, in my twenties I began to notice changes occurring in society; changes for the worse, a decline in the interrelations between people, between couples and also individually. Divorces have become much more prevalent, the number of single-parent households has been increasing steadily, there's more infidelity, the caring about oneself more than the 'two' or the family unit, sex has begun to take centre stage in people's lives and women have started gradually to become less and less feminine. This decline perhaps began in the early 20th century, but started to become exponentially worse some twenty years ago, paralleling and almost certainly due to, the inception and expansion of the internet and the steep rise in technological advancements and the use of them.

I, attempting to look at things from a broader perspective, began to feel very conscious and wary of these changes. Furthermore, almost everyone I'd spoken with shared similar sentiments yet could not say what and who exactly were to be blamed for them. Nor could they tell what should be done about it and how to go about doing it. Worse of all, they simply went along, often with great pain and perturbation. It felt like an uncontrollable force, led by an unknown, was leading us all on a premeditated course to an obscure place or future. Nevertheless, I have always believed that people are basically good and that they are capable of change. I couldn't help but try to do something about it and decided to raise these matters with as many people as I could. I offered my opinions and my observations to those I came into contact with about why I thought society was going in the direction that it was, and also tried to provide them with some encouragement to remain strong and true to their beliefs and to preserve their integrity as much as possible.

These subjects could reasonably be placed under the heading of relationships. Femininity, this classic trait of women, may not at first glance seem to have much to do with relationships, yet in my opinion it is a majorly important aspect that is involved and intertwined with all interactions between women and men. Both 'relationships' and 'femininity' separately and conjointly have been suffering heavy blows of late. I decided to write this book because these subjects are dear to me and in my view form part of a very small group of fundamental ingredients which are needed to maintain a sane and workable culture and civilization. This book is chiefly dedicated to these two subjects.

Femininity to me is a form of art and it represents beauty, grace, creation, profound intimacy and life. Women are basically beautiful creatures without whom the world we live in would be a very dull place. A woman's love can be complete and overwhelming, filled with devotion and dedication, and it is often unconditional. Women are the calming factor in a world riddled with conflict, altercations and uneasiness. They generally are the proof of the basic goodness of human beings and of what the future of humanity can be were it to embrace the attitudes and perspectives women possess. Given all of what I believe, I couldn't not have become very concerned about the changes society has been through during the last two or three decades with regards to these topics.

I am romantic and optimistic in nature. Since I can remember I've always looked at life through a relatively wide lens which has become even wider as I've grown older. I've always loved to converse with people, to listen to their ideas, feelings, dreams and life stories. When I engage in conversations, when it is appropriate, I offer my opinions and ideas drawn from experience and what I consider logic and rationality. I feel that I have a lot to say and give advice about and I always make sure it is constructive and positive, aimed at evoking right and just action in order to better the listener's situation, her/his life and/or the people involved. Helping people in any capacity has always given me great pleasure. I have had hundreds upon hundreds of conversations with individuals around the world, but these happening once or twice a week, as inspirational and beneficial as they may be to some, were not going to make a major difference in the world and reverse the decline with respect to the subjects in question.

I would like, however, to apologize in advance for some of the content in this book, for it may at times sound pessimistic and somewhat bitter. This was not my intention; these are my observations and the way I view matters as they have been and currently are. My love for people is greater than my feelings of disappointment and anger towards them. I hope that my observations and opinions will strike a chord with you. As I said, I am optimistic in nature and always will be. I believe in the goodness of people and their ability to better themselves and even change.

We all like to interact, converse, smile; give and receive a kind word, a hug or a kiss. Perhaps if we could act more maturely and objectively and lower our guard and walls a little and trust our fellow humans a little more we would then stop hurting them and be hurt less in return.

I would like to note that a few of the concepts talked about in this book are not mine. I merely adopted them and chose to write about them in my own words and from my own perspectives.

I wish for your journey with me through this book to be a pleasurable one. One that may reaffirm what you've already known but couldn't or didn't really have the chance to utter or articulate. A journey that will inspire you, even if just a little, to a better life for yourself and the people around you.

What is a female?

The best and most natural place to begin a book about femininity would be by defining what a woman fundamentally is.

This is the definition of a female in the Merriam Webster dictionary followed by another definition of an important term:

"Of, relating to, or being the sex that typically has the capacity to bear young or produce eggs".

Chromosomes are where all our genetic code resides. Each out of 46 chromosomes holds a number of different genes responsible for different things in our bodies.

Chromosomes all reside inside the cell. Each and every cell contains them.

In order to understand the very basic definition of a female we must look deeply into our bodies and cells.

Do not be alarmed! This book will not deal with technical information at all. Bear with me through only a few more pieces of data.

We all have 23 pairs of chromosomes, a total of 46. Two of the 46, one pair, are sex chromosomes and they determine the sex of the individual. Basically, only one chromosome will be different from a woman to a man. Two X sex chromosomes in the cells of a female, and one X and one Y in a man's.

A female egg, which contains only the X sex chromosome is fertilized by a male sperm and the sex of the child is then determined. When the male sperm contains a Y chromosome the baby will be a boy; when it contains an X chromosome it will be a girl.

Female is the term given to a person whose cells contain only X sex chromosomes. These chromosomes exist in every cell of her body. That is the very basic definition of a female.

By the way, one chromosome out of 46 may not sound so much but it is responsible for plenty of distinctions between women and men. Plenty of the genes inside these sex chromosomes act differently in women and men determining many differences between the genders. Apart from these genes inside of the sex chromosomes, many genes inside other chromosomes differ in their activities from women to men.

Which brings us to:

Differences

There are two distinguished biological genders on this planet. Let us in this chapter name several of the obvious and important differences between the two: women and men.

Different to women, men cannot bear children and do not lactate. Men are generally taller, have wider shoulders, heads and necks, are more masculine and have more hair on their faces and bodies. Men have penises and flat breasts, men lose their hair quicker, men are fertile all their lives, men s Adam's apples are bigger, they have deeper voices and men get fat in different parts of the body.

Other major but less obvious differences may include:

- Men are more prone to most diseases. Women live longer.

- Internal organs differ in size from women to men.

- Skeletal structure is not the same for both genders.

- Men are colour blind much more frequently than women.

- Women generally have a greater body fat percentage than men.

There are numerous other biological differences from oxygen uptake – the amount of oxygen the body requires for certain activities – through vein size to hormone levels and functions. Clearly, biological systems, organs, tissues and functions would differ from a body rigged to bear children to one that is not.

There are around twenty thousand genes comprising and constructing our bodies. Close to a whopping number of six thousand vary from women to men.

This presentation of distinctions between the genders brings me to the point I'm trying to make;

Imagine a world where everyone looks alike? It would be awful, wouldn't it!? Just like a demoralizing futuristic film. Imagine ten people in your place of work or neighbourhood looking exactly like you, like they were your identical twin. Or a thousand people in your city who have the same exact character as you, how would that make you feel? It would be terrible if we weren't different from the person next to us, wouldn't it? Certainly it would. We can even sometimes get a bit displeased when someone in the room with us or two others at work have the same name as ours. Fortunately, we are all different in so many ways.

We all want to be special in a way, to have our own unique physical and personal features, to have our own individual minds, our own taste with regards to different things, our own opinions and idiosyncrasies. We all want to be viewed and taken as unique individuals with a distinctive set of characteristics. Think of it! Not many things are worse than being and looking like everybody else. Picture millions of people who look and behave exactly like you flooding this world… If that were to happen that would mean that you are no longer an individual, that you have nothing unique or special to say, to give or to offer, that you are completely predictable. That would be one miserable reality! We don't think about things of this sort often, but we nonetheless knowingly and unknowingly doing things for the purpose of setting us apart from others.

The purpose of this paragraph is to show that differences should be celebrated. To be too different from one another won't be conducive to any group of people or a society. But dissimilarities are essential for good and interesting living. Not many things in this world are more dissimilar than women and men.

The differences between women and men are fundamental. Apart from the biological distinctions, the very basic attitudes, approaches and viewpoints to just about anything are dissimilar. Biological and social factors determine these dissimilarities. In general, women are more sensitive, are more emotionally intelligent, more astute, more mature, rational, patient, composed and less aggressive. Women are basically feminine, they are gentler and more graceful.

Women are able to bear children, this is probably the biggest and most dramatic difference between the sexes. There will be a huge difference in the perception of life across the boards between a person who is able to conceive and bring life into existence, and one who is not.

Both a woman and a man are necessary in order to create new life but it can be said that women are the ones blessed with the gift of giving life!

This major biological difference between the genders is also a mental and psychological one. Women are more likely to feel like the soul guardian for future generations.

Therefore, the fundamental approaches of women and men to the subject of conception and pregnancy, the subject of creating life, vary greatly. Almost every sexual intercourse can traditionally, biologically and historically mean conception to a woman. Her life can change in a split second, another human being can be created. Were she to conceive, the child would be growing inside of her for nine long months. Men obviously do not go through that. This somewhat long process requires waiting and patience. A man has no physical and biological duties after the act of sex. The responsibility of the woman is much greater. She gives one egg that can then grow into a human being, which she knows for certain will be raised by her – we can't state the same level of certainty in the case of the father. She is thus more prudent and cautious with regards to sex and pregnancy and consequently also more selective in the choice of her partners. More on that and on other distinctions between the sexes later on.

Biological – psychological

The differences in women's and men's biological systems and organs of reproduction have a great influence on the way the genders think, behave and perceive life and living. The fact that women are being penetrated and men penetrate makes all the difference in the world. It is a much bigger invasion of one's space, body and privacy when one is being penetrated as compared to the one doing the penetration. Something is going inside of her body. We are generally quite possessive, sensitive and shy concerning our internal spaces. That is one of the reasons why rape is such an awful thing.

Perhaps due to the fact that a woman is being penetrated – her space is being breached and by being a little more passive concerning the act of sex she is compensated for it in the matters preceding the act – she makes the decision whether to let someone in or not, and the choosing of the person who will be let in. This is only logical when we also consider the fact that an egg is really choosy and selective with regards to the sperm it lets in. It is only natural that a woman will be the one chased by men or men 'swimming' towards her and thus be the one who chooses whom to let in. It seems as though the whole subject of ladylikeness and gentlemanliness was basically decided for us by nature.

Owing to the reasons above, the physical and therefore also psychological consequences are more impactful and profound for the penetrated party. This is one of the reasons why a woman needs to trust a man first before she lets him in, literally and metaphorically.

This particular difference also makes women more self-conscious, much more so in most instances. Women are the sought-after sex and the ones who carry the responsibility of choosing the right one wisely. As a result, they look inwards more and more often, by definition being more self-conscious. Being pursued is a very different role to being the pursuer, the ways one acts and behaves change accordingly.

Furthermore, the more one is supposed to be active when it comes to the search for and the act of sex (he is the one who needs to persuade the woman to agree to have sex. Also, he is the one who's doing the actual physical action, penetrating), the more one will search for it and the more one will be obsessed with the need and desire to have it. It is one of the reasons why women are less compulsive about sex and less impulsive with regards to it.

Another major difference – and a very interesting fact too – is that the male sperm divides into two different types, possessing different characteristics: the type that contains the Y chromosome – which produces a male offspring, swims faster, is more erratic and also dies sooner than the X male chromosome which produces a female offspring. The X chromosome sperm is more resilient and lives longer. It is quite remarkable. We can easily see how these biological differences could to a degree be exhibited in life and character, influencing the behaviour of the two genders.

Every woman out there is familiar with the level of anxiety men can possess when it comes to sexual intercourse, in a way similar to the anxiety of the male-producing sperm. Even more fundamental to the behaviour of the male-producing sperm is the fact that women produce one egg (sometimes two) once a month. That egg then sits there waiting, being neither assertive nor anxious; it seems to be in no rush and on top of all that, picky and selective when it's time to let a single sperm merge with it. Men on the other hand *constantly* produce sperm and in the act of sex cast millions of sperm (more than two hundred million, in fact) in order for one of them to fertilize the egg, as if it were a numbers game and the more we cast the better chances we have to impregnate a woman. It's as though men are subconsciously and continuously being driven to have sexual intercourse with woman. This, combined with the great feeling of relief and enjoyment that accompany men's ejaculation and the fact that men are the ones who are supposed to penetrate, means we can see how that particular man's biology can affect him in character and mind in various ways, especially in the way he perceives the act of sex and the pursuit of it and women.

This need, or urge, makes men less rational, less composed and more aggressive; when an urge is constantly pushing against a person, no matter how lightly, that person is likely to be less patient and composed than a person who doesn't have that constantly pressing urge. Men are very impatient when it comes to sex and the need to ejaculate. Impatience and lack of composure are key prerequisites for becoming aggressive. Any incessant urge or impulse will cripple a person to a degree. Sex will definitely succeed in doing so.

Men are victims of their own biology to some extent. But this is no excuse for many of the things men are rightly accused of by women.

More differences between the sexes

Enjoyment and trust

The vast majority of women need to feel something towards a man in order to be with him sexually. After some affinity has been established and she has had sex with him, to really enjoy the act she normally needs even more time to better get to know him; to trust him more. Only then can she be there completely, in the moment and let herself really enjoy. Even if a couple's first time together in bed is great, it will get even better the more the woman trusts the man. Most men, on the other hand, are not very particular about whom they have sex with; affection and emotion are not prerequisites for sexual intercourse.

At the beginning of the relationship and as long as she does not fully trust the man, a woman, before, during and after having sex can be somewhat disconnected and pensive, she could be worrying about an array of things. This will of course change when trust sets in.

Men are normally not pensive at all before, during and after the act. They may be, but only to the extent that they are concerned with whether they perform well or not. Men too will enjoy sex better after some time has passed but this is mainly thanks to the woman, who is now feeling more relaxed and trusting.

Perceptions

Our perspectives on life and living change according to our biology, physique, duties, responsibilities, character, fortunes and misfortunes; in short, the sum total of the factors comprising our lives. Women's perspectives are thus very different to men's; their outlook on life, understanding of it and the profundity of it are all different to varying degrees. A woman's thought processes often differ from men's. Which is also why women and men diverged from one another on their levels of romanticism, with women being normally more romantic. More on that later on.

Women are happier and more contented generally. The average woman smiles more than the average man. Men have a shorter attention span. Women, having a longer attention span, can listen and focus better. It is remarkable to see when looking at an average couple sitting in a restaurant, for example, how the woman's attention is more focused on the man and the things in front of her, she is present in mind, but the men's attention is often more dispersed. This can often easily be noticed by an astute observer looking at the man's eyes which are often moving about in a somewhat endless and aimless search. I feel for men; I am one, I know what it feels like to be constantly pressured by biological and sociological elements which are not under your full control. There seems to be an underlying uneasiness in men stemming from their biological composition and socially acquired attributes.

I do not think that the differences in attention span and the ability to focus from women to men are always big and noticeable. Many men can be very attentive and focused and as good as or better than some women. These abilities are strictly mental and are thus very individualistic but they can nonetheless, like anything else, be influenced by biology and sociology. As a general rule, women score more points on that subject also.

Due to all of the above – the biological rationale and the superiority of the female gender being feminine, graceful and aesthetic (to be discussed at length in the next chapter) – women came to symbolize and represent an object of desire to men, something to pursue, something that men are anxious to have and need to make an effort in order to get, and thus something greatly appreciated. Anxiety on the part of men to have a woman is a funny and interesting notion when you consider the fact that fifty percent of the population are women and there is one for every man. Men should thus not be so anxious to get one, but they are. Men feel very unsettled when they do not have a woman.

Alone

Another intriguing phenomenon is that men are not as good at being alone as women are. Men cannot handle being alone and loneliness as well as women.

Goals and purposes are the fuels that keep our fire and passion burning. Life without goals or purposes is like a car put in neutral moving along a slightly downward inclined surface until we're forty and then the surface straightens and we can barely move forward anymore. It can often be underestimated but the fact that a woman can have a life grow inside her – from one small cell to a whole human being; nourished, fed and protected until birth when it is brought into the world and then raised by her – will understandably give her a real or potentially real sense of purpose and meaning in life. Bringing new life into the world is such an important matter for us humans that when one really thinks about it one realizes that without it there is no future and the whole natural and taken almost for granted existence of the human race would cease to be.

The mere fact that she knows she can bring life, to have and to hold and to be near and close to, will give her some comfort in life. A person's livelihood depends greatly on the level of assistance and help she/he offers others. To bring a new person into existence and to tend and care for it until years later is a great deal of help.

It would then undoubtedly be easier for a woman to handle being alone and hardship in life. The more purposeful a 20 person is, the more she/he can and does contribute to and help others, the more accomplished, relaxed and satisfied that person is likely to feel and therefore less susceptible to feeling alone or lonely. Women's basic disposition is different to men's. Women can obviously be unhappy, depressed and melancholy but they are normally more at ease and comfortable in their own skin than men. They thus have less tendency to depression and are generally more contented in life

Moreover, men historically were never alone. They usually had someone to be with and take care of them, sometimes more than one. Women, on the other hand, not having as much control over their lives as men, were alone most of the time, even when they had husbands and children. They were left alone and often neglected and thus had had more opportunity to learn how to live by themselves. In addition, up until recently, most cultures were chauvinist and patriarchal, meaning that men used to hold arrogant and condescending attitudes towards women that prevented them from really trying – or having the patience to try – to understand women, thus women were never fully understood. When you're not fully understood or there is no real attempt to understand you, you won't truly feel that the person you're with is wholly with you. Due to the different natures and types of lives women and men had, it was very hard for men to understand the female psyche even when they did try.

No matter how close to you a person is physically or how many hours a day he/she spends with you, if that person does not really understand you and you cannot talk about anything and everything and share your emotions and thoughts with him/her you will, fairly quickly, feel a little bit alone. There will be a part of you that he/she can't understand, reach or touch, so this part will remain only within you, you won't be able to genuinely share it. The less you are being understood the bigger the void and the more alone you'll feel. Many women know what that feels like. You are close to a person to the degree that you can share things and have an understanding with that person.

That did indeed contribute or cause, if you will, women to be able to live in their own worlds, with themselves, partly alone. They have pretty much got used to it and have come to not expect too much from men in that regard.

Together with the powerful ability to bring life, this makes loneliness and being alone more manageable for women.

Forgiveness

Women are also more forgiving and understanding.

Women can often forgive a betrayal by their man and put it behind them. Understanding the weaknesses men suffer from and realizing that staying together – giving another chance to the relationship and keeping the family intact – are more important in the grand scheme of things. Women have a much more future-oriented outlook on life than men.

Women are also more forgiving or accepting when it comes to thoughts and fantasies about other women on the part of men. Women are wise to and very much used to men's perverse and erratic minds when it comes to sex, such that they don't even resent it that much anymore; most of them accept it to be the nature of men and learn to live with it. Another issue women almost automatically compromise on.

Men usually are much less able to think straight when the shoe is on the other foot, when their woman cheats or fantasizes about someone else. Men get filled with anger and with a feeling of helplessness, and are slow in forgetting and forgiving. Most men cannot even support the thought that their woman might think of someone else, look in his direction, let alone fantasize about him.

Women have had a lot of practice coping with men's fantasies and thoughts about other women throughout history, unfortunately. Their expectations of men are usually not very high and their understanding of men is profound. All things considered, romantic women (more than average) will not stand for that behaviour, good on them. I wish many more would do the same.

Cause and effect

The whole subject of human interactions and interrelations, the success or failure of them, is based on two concepts, two basic modes of *being* and the balance between them. They are 'cause' and 'effect'. 'cause' would mean having control or power over, to instigate or initiate a doingness, to make something happen and making sure things go the way you intend. 'Effect' would mean being controlled, directed or influenced by, to be more the result of something, an action or someone. It can also mean passivity: going along with things, occurrences or people even when you don't want or like to. When one is waiting for something to occur one is being passive, 'effect'. When one is taking charge of situations and life one is being active, 'cause'. When a husband makes most of the decisions in the family his wife is bearing the results of those decisions, hence she is the 'effect' of them, the 'effect' of her husband. He is more 'cause' than her in their relationship.

These two concepts determine the makeup of any interaction and relationship. Our perception on how balanced these two concepts should be and how we practice them in life determines the amount of respect, love, appreciation and just about any emotion we can have towards ourselves and others. When a person is being a complete 'effect'; the result of other people's actions or wants, situations or things, does not preserve his integrity from fear of resistance, being passive in the face of hardship and obstacles – basically he has no control over life, then it will be practically impossible for that person to get anywhere in life, to attain any of his goals and aspirations nor will he be respected, appreciated or truly loved – we find it difficult to respect and love someone who doesn't respect him/herself. When a person is being 'cause' more often than 'effect' – working at or towards something until she/he achieves it or overcomes it, keeps her/his integrity, speaks her/his mind, not being passive and docile because of social pressure or trends – then that person will be habitually respected and appreciated and will normally succeed in life. Obviously, there are also bad ways of being 'cause' but these will not normally get you very far in life.

Given the biological composition of a female, women are more 'effect' than 'cause' in a couple of significant areas of life: bearing children and also with respect to force. The nature of this planet and its elements mean that much has to be solid, strong and stable; therefore, many things require force to be built, operated on or simply to be carried or moved. With regard to children-rearing, a woman, as mentioned, is indeed responsible for most of the process from conception to birth, but there are still some factors in and during this process that make her more an 'effect' than 'cause'. She has a very small window of opportunity to get pregnant. She ovulates for only thirty-six hours a month, having normally produced only one egg for potential reproduction which can at times be infertile. Men on the other hand can constantly produce life-creating substance, any minute of the day any day of the month. This makes women more open to internal and external criticism, upset and disappointment. In addition, once a woman becomes pregnant she is then physically vulnerable and weaker than usual for the duration of the pregnancy. And, given her strong emotional connection with her offspring, she is also more emotionally vulnerable and can thus be more easily affected and manipulated by ill-intentioned people.

A woman is more 'effect' than 'cause' during all this process.

Force-wise, when a home to live in needs to be erected, a kitchen to be built or a heavy bed to be moved, among many other things, generally men are required for the job. When a war is waging a woman is at the mercy of men. Women, of course, are and can be 'cause' in many other aspects of life, we're getting there…

Due to the physique of women it was also decreed upon us that men will be slightly more 'cause' or active in the act of sex itself. And thanks to the physique of women and them being feminine, it was almost unanimously agreed that men would be gentlemen – meaning more things will be done for women and not the other way around, supposedly making women a little more 'effect' than 'cause' in that respect as well. I say supposedly because, even though being 'cause' is generally better than being 'effect', there are instances when 'effect' is preferable. More on that later.

Women being more 'effect' than 'cause' in the above-mentioned matters is in large part the basis for the *recent* and over-the-edge feminist movement in many parts of the world (more on which is coming…).

There are two sexes on this planet and possibly in the universe. That is how nature was created. One was chosen to be able to bear children and one was not. One was chosen to biologically be more masculine, stronger, and one not as masculine and not as strong physically. Roughly, men use their muscles more often, women use more gentleness. Also, one was chosen to have the organ with which to penetrate and one to be penetrated. This is what nature gave us. Thought processes change according to biology to an extent and are made automatically and subconsciously most of the time. The mind, the spirit, i.e. the person, acts more like a woman or more like a man when it is in a woman's or man's body respectively. For instance, having a child growing in you will definitely provide you with a perspective different to the one a person who cannot bear children will have. When one is more masculine and has more physical strength, one's attitudes and approaches towards things and life will differ from a person who is not as strong physically. Femininity, then, could not really have been a male feature, not with his physiological and biological composition. A person can choose, in a way, to behave in one way more than the other, yet for thousands of years people chose basically to work with and adapt to the biological tools they had inherited. Meaning that most women choose not to do work which requires heavy lifting, for example. Women, being more cause than men in other compartments of life suggests that 'cause' and 'effect' can and should work together, complement and balance each other; nature apparently meant for this to be so.

'Cause' and 'effect' do not always mean good or bad, better or worse and the difference between them does not have to be big at all. Recently, we have tended to think that being 'cause' – in charge of things, the one who initiates and instigates things – is much, much better than to be an 'effect' – on the receiving end of things. People look down on being an 'effect' and consider it to be weak – not all people, of course, but a growing number nonetheless and especially the modern woman – given the history of our cultures up until recent times this is understandable to a degree.

But, this type of thinking or attitude is unfortunate and false. Being the 'effect' of something does not necessarily make us the weak one; when one CHOOSES to be 'effect' one is actually being strong. To be able to receive and, more importantly, let the other person be 'cause' means strength, and these are two abilities which are crucial to the mental health of our society (excluding bad and harmful ways of being cause and effect). This means that the appearance of 'cause' and 'effect' is mostly and merely an appearance and that in actuality 'effect' can be also 'cause' and vice versa. That tells us that what and how one FEELS with regards to an action or doingness determines whether one was the 'effect' or 'cause' of it or both together and to what degree.

The degrees and ratio of 'cause' and 'effect' between two people are determined by their ability, desire and agreement to be either and their understanding of this mechanism. One chooses to be 'cause' or 'effect'; you choose to let him/her be 'cause' thus choosing to be 'effect' and, most importantly, when you let another be 'cause' and yourself the 'effect' in actuality and practically you're also being 'cause' at the same time! You chose to be the effect of something or someone; you are the one who made that decision. When one answers the phone, one CHOOSES to be an 'effect'; to receive communication. One chooses to let the person on the end of the line initiate a conversation, to be cause. Balanced levels of 'cause' and 'effect' will be the best way to go about things and most beneficial for any two people in a relationship.

Women, up until recent times and still in some cultures today, have normally been more 'effect' than 'cause' in most areas of life – mainly because that is what had been decided for them by patriarchal and chauvinist societies. In an objective world, more like today's, 'cause' and 'effect' are more a matter of choice, in most subjects.

There has to be a balance, though; in society today, women try to be more and more cause and less and less effect. This is very disadvantageous to us all. The law of conservation of energy can be applied here as well; we can't have one person becoming more cause without the other becoming more effect. More on women and men in today's world later on.

Other contributors

Let's name some other sociological and historical factors that have contributed to and are also responsible for these differences between the genders, as well as elaborating on those just mentioned:

Given the bloody, force-based history of this planet, men, being the strongest sex physically, were the natural candidates to become the protectors of future generations, providing a safe environment for their pregnant wives and children for many centuries. Vigilance and toughness then became second nature to men. Moreover, the fact that a man needed to work, provide for his family, run towns, cities and countries from philosophical and administrative matters through to the most physical labour duties, as well as from time to time going to war, made it harder for him to focus on and enjoy the finer things in life and experience the beautiful and gentler side of it, like intimacy, togetherness – as in romanticism and the raising of children. That state of affairs kept man looking outward most of the time, constantly busy with the physical world around him, as opposed to his inside world, making it difficult for him to learn about himself except for the lessons learnt through aggression and hard work, which can be very rewarding and revealing but wouldn't appeal to the softer and gentler side of him. As people we possess the whole spectrum of human emotions and potential mental attributes and capabilities. Both women and men are capable of experiencing them all.

Under these circumstances it would have been very tough for men to develop emotional intelligence to a level higher than that required to win battles or manipulate other men in trade, politics and so on.

That statement does not fully apply to the men who engaged in art and philosophy. I say not fully, because even such men usually suffered from a superiority complex over women which made them want to remain different to women and keep some distance from 'womanly' features and practices; they wouldn't therefore introvert and engage in introspection to the level that women were forced to.

On the other hand, a woman lived a different reality on account of her physical and social inferiority and her dependency on her husband's physical, political and social strengths and powers, plus the fact that he used to be the head of the family and the main provider who kept her and her children alive. She was, most of the time, oppressed and suppressed by a very prejudiced society, a society controlled and ruled by men – from petty matters to those of the highest significance that could influence her whole life and livelihood. She was mostly regarded as a second-rate citizen and often used for sexual purposes by men and as a servant. Thus, she had no choice but introversion and introspection. Accordingly, she would devise and learn better and wiser ways to enhance her and her children's survival chances and quality of life in this man's world that she had absolutely no control over. She naturally became more astute and, in turn, conceived of finer psychological and emotional ways to express herself, achieve what she wanted and also for interacting with others. She would understand herself better; her reactions, her emotional and psychological dispositions, and consequently became more sensitive to people's and children's emotions and needs. She would tend, care for and occupy herself with the more delicate aspects of life, like bearing and raising children.

Often working at home waiting for her husband to come back from work, at times for days or weeks – and sometimes from war – she had a lot of time to contemplate life, look within, learn about herself and develop her attitudes, approaches and emotional intelligence according to her circumstances and situations. She would not engage in war and her world would not revolve around aggression. She would develop a finer sensitivity to human suffering, inequalities, wrongdoing and discomfort. She would be more intelligent emotionally.

The mere fact that she knew that there was someone who could hurt her, subjugate her, silence her and change her life the way he or they saw fit, and that she could do nothing about it, more than any other factor, truly made the difference and was the predominant reason why she would introvert and introspect and become all that she has become. There is a huge difference between living in relative control and living in relative fear with little control over your person and livelihood. It changes the way you feel, think, act and, eventually, who you are.

Aware of these differences and advantages they have over men, women often bemoan the lack of ability on the part of men to be as profound as they are. Fairly early in life they discover that men are incapable of truly understanding them. Ordinarily, most men become very predictable to women. I can see this in the eyes of most women when the subjects of love and relationships come up. When women reach a certain age, usually after several or many encounters with men and attempts at relationships, despondency is clear, compromise has become second nature to them. Some have forsaken their ideals, their dream romance, their dream man. Some simply lower their standards and others have given up on the idea altogether. (Many men have too, but hope for both is not lost! More on that later on).

As an aside, I'm certain that if women were in charge of our world there would be far fewer wars (if any), conflicts, atrocities and suffering; a lot less bloodshed and loss of life and limb.

Commitment

On a purely psychological/mental basis, men are as capable of commitment as women are. Alas, when the above-mentioned biological and historical differences come into play, which they have from the beginning of our bodies' evolution, we again get divergence and women take the upper hand here as well. In my opinion, most influential is the biological rationale which implies that commitment is ingrained in a woman; the long process of creating life inside her and the very long one afterwards of raising and caring for it. Committing is basically in her nature. Second, many of the practices observed historically by men living in patriarchal societies – quite a few of which were anti-commitment practices – have continued in use to this day.

Another distinction between the sexes: Cheating

Another big difference between the genders although diminishing of late is that men cheat much more and their reasons for doing so are quite different to those of women.

One of the underlying causes for that would be the biological nature of men discussed earlier – the constant production of sperm, the constant readiness; that need to spread one's seed. Moreover, the 'numbers game' mentioned above very likely plays a part: millions of sperm cells trying to get to one egg, possibly influencing men on a subconscious level to make more attempts at impregnating a woman. That can easily lead to attempting to be with more than just one woman; the more-the-better-chance-we-have type of approach. In general, a man's body is anxious to plant another seed, life-giving sperm, to create life. Men's bodies – biologically and therefore to a degree also on a subconscious level – believe that this pushes death further away from them, makes them less mortal. There is an extraordinary push on the part of the body to create life so that future generations will exist, so life can be continued.

But these factors are not the main reason why men cheat; they merely act as stimuli, agitators and justifiers. The main reason men cheat is their *lack of ability to find meaning in life and their being insecure.* Some cheat because they are looking for excitement, some like to be secretive and lead a double life and some just because it is ok and almost accepted today as a norm, especially amongst men. But the search for meaning is key, as is insecurity, and these can manifest themselves in various ways. Let's look at men's search for or lack of meaning in life, as one leads to the other – insecurity.

We as humans don't really know why we are alive, here on this world and what the purpose and meaning for all of that are. We are all dumbfounded with regards to these mysteries to a degree, and the search for answers has been a major human endeavour from the beginning of time. One thing has always been clear though: when a person has a purpose, an obstacle to overcome, a dream she/he is after or a major goal, life to that person has more meaning, makes more sense. Men generally find it harder than women to make sense of life, to find meaning or to appreciate life. Especially at times of rest when men have no big goals, problems or obstacles to face. Women are born with an innate partial sense and meaning of life; the ability to bring life into the world. It gives them a sense of purpose, an important one too – whether they realize it or not. Although it is not everything in life nor is it the most, it is nevertheless a lot, much more than what men are innately endowed with.

Therefore, a man needs to find ways to compensate for that inability to grow and bring life into the world in order to make more sense of things or life. When he doesn't have specific goals and purposes in life he finds himself looking for meaning and sense elsewhere. The closest and best place to look for these is with other people. When people –

living creatures like himself – give him love or attention; more affirmation that he is needed and wanted, such as when a woman wants him, basically showing they want to be with him or around him, that person feels more alive; more wanted and needed, life then makes more sense, has a little more meaning and he will appreciate it more. While for the vast majority of women – and also for many men – one spouse or a family is enough to make some sense of life, for many men it is not, the void is too big. Thus, they seek attention from more people and for obvious reasons a very good place to feel loved, needed and wanted would be with the opposite sex. This can of course be regarded as immature behaviour stemming from insecurity, which it is. That is why men are often childish, less mature than women and require more attention.

The more purposeful a person's life is (positive purposes), the less likely that person is to look for validation and attention elsewhere and the less likely he/she is to cheat.

Furthermore, cultures in the past, being mostly patriarchal, meant that many men, definitely not all, could and did indeed have more than one woman in their lives for thousands of years. This provided them with the extra attention and 'love' they needed in order to make some sense of their lives. It made them feel somewhat in control, look cool and popular amongst their peers which in turn, of course, made men feel good about themselves. Thus, men's attention was often scattered and directed at more than one woman; men would look at, think of and make advances to other women, practices that are still shared by many today.

One of these practices or attitudes is this unspoken kind of contest that exists between men: who will score more and who has had more women. This rationale applies mainly to young males (but not only): the more you score, the more popular you are among your friends. They are just being juvenile and silly. It goes without saying that not all young men are like this, but this mentality and some other historically inherited attitudes have seeped through the ages and are still prevalent, having an impact on the minds of plenty of men today.

That brings us to the natural offshoot of the lower sense of existence and meaning in life: insecurity – uncertainty or anxiety about oneself or one's life. One of the main and awesome catalysts of that insecurity, and why older men cheat, is the fear of dying. Yes, they are afraid of death. When one is born with fundamental and unanswered questions concerning life and the after-life, compounded by a lowly sense of existence and meaning, and later one sees time ticking away with the end of life approaching, fear of death becomes doubly accentuated.

The less one finds meaning in one's life, the more one would be insecure and the more one would fear death. The less one contributes to life and the living, the more one would dread dying.

By being with another woman or more women, men try to feel a little more alive or alive again, to feel less insecure, to push death away: "I still have it"; "I can still conquer a woman"; "I'm not too old for that"; "another woman likes me, wants me".

Dating a younger or much younger woman is an excellent example of men's fear of death or their not coming to terms with the fact that they will die one day. Like, for example, the practice common among many men: getting a divorce and marrying a younger woman. By dating a younger woman, men can try to regain youth or a younger age. They try to live vicariously through that woman's age, age-related behaviour and looks. Obviously, that this is at all possible is due to the fact that many women, for various reasons, are ok with dating older men. Often, they need to. Being more mature than the average man does not leave them with much choice.

In addition, the fact that most men would cheat and not disclose it – keep it a secret – substantiates their need to massage their egos and deal a blow to their demons of insecurity; having two women interested in them, desire them. There is also the appeal of leading a secret life, like in the movies, but that argument is more of a justification one makes to oneself to mask the real issue here, which is insecurity.

Women worry about and fear death much less than men, through the same reasoning that enables them to handle being alone better. In all likelihood, it is thanks to the ability to give life that they possess: that meaningful and profound deed of creation that they do or are capable of doing. That makes them generally calmer, more appreciative of life and the living, and more fulfilled as people. Most possibly that is why they also live longer and normally suffer from less afflictions than men.

When one has done really well in one's lifetime, done some meaningful things, achieved good things and/or helped people, one feels good about oneself, about one's contribution to people and/or the environment or even the world. That person would then be more relaxed and less afraid when his/her time comes. I believe that bearing children, motherhood, is a big enough deed to make women feel good enough about their contribution to life and society. We, men, have a lot more to do in order to feel accomplished in relation to ourselves and our input to society.

Women traditionally represent the better side of humanity; they usually cheat only when cheated on or treated badly. They are a living proof that humans are basically monogamous, romantic and devoted.

Look to the woman

Take away testosterone and the obsession on the part of men to have sex, his aggression and violent inclinations, and the world would instantly rise to a whole different level. Criminals, rapists, warmongers are almost exclusively men. Men's appreciation of life is generally less than that of women's; which is perhaps why many of them have engaged in war and stupid, violent games for millennia. It is only logical that some men would attempt to fill these voids of lowered sense of existence and meaning in life, plus their insecurity, by searching for conquest and even through extreme violence. Or perhaps it is merely a reaction, a retort for not having that fulfilling and sought-after feeling of having meaning in life.

Furthermore, when one is insecure – which can lead to unhappiness among other things – one is more likely to become aggressive. Men are also more prone to depression and suicide than women. All these things and more tell me one thing and one thing only: when it comes to the true human character and optimal behaviour, look to the woman. It is a very simple and logical choice.

All things considered, there are lots of calm, relaxed and loyal men in the world. All that is written here is general in nature and serves to emphasize some of the basic differences between the sexes.

With all that in mind, let us move forward and examine the essence of women.

Femininity

(in its truest sense)

"Blessed are you, ruler of the universe who has not created me a woman." I first thought about this and uttered that line when I was 26. I really meant it then and I really mean it now. My life could have been much less interesting if I had been born a girl. And the reason is, being a man, I have something to admire, look up to in many ways, chase after, appreciate!

I feel a little bit sorry for women; there is generally much less to admire in men, unfortunately. Men can be appreciated, loved, respected and even adored, and indeed, many men are amazing people, deserving of commendation. But in general, as a gender, men are normally less praiseworthy than women.

To me the main thing to admire in women has always been femininity.

What is femininity? What does it mean to be feminine?

First, let's have a look at some dictionary definitions of feminine:

Merriam Webster: "the quality or nature of the female sex"

Oxford dictionaries: "qualities or attributes regarded as characteristic of women"

Google: "the quality of being female; womanliness"

True, femininity is a feature and quality of women, but none of these definitions truly gives us a sense of what femininity really is.

The dictionaries merely declare, 'woman-like', 'quality of the female sex'.

No definition explains what it is in actuality.

Let's examine what femininity really is, what it means in terms of behaviour, feelings, perception, attitude, movement and even thought.

Femininity *in its truest sense* is an innate but mostly acquired quality and it is as close to art as humanly possible!

At the dawn of time when creation occurred, two genders emerged. One gender, the male, was created more masculine, with more strength, 'chosen' to be the tough, rough, more physical executer of things, while the other was chosen be able to give life and to be the more delicate and gentler one.

But what is this quality?

Everything we do in life involves motion, life is motion. Even inside of us motion is constantly occurring – in each and every part of our body from the smallest particle inside a cell to the largest organ. There is constant motion all around us as well. Living requires motion.

Some motion is happening on a very small scale, tiny magnitudes which are invisible to the naked eye but we can still often see the results of that motion. When we look at a beautiful flower or a painting, for example, we see them in the way that their particles – atoms, molecules, structure, which are motion – are arranged. It is motion that appears still, inanimate to us.

Other kinds of motion we are easily capable of seeing. These evidently have an appearance to us – they have movement, shape, form – like a snowflake falling, a flower blowing in the wind, a car moving, the way we walk, move, use hand gestures, speak, etc…

We, humans, are capable of evaluating things, to conceive of ideas and concepts, to reason, to think and have preferences and taste. Thus, we regard some types of motion as beautiful and others ugly, as well as anything in between.

We generally agree on what is beautiful and what is ugly. There are some basic agreements about beauty and the perception of it, which we all share: straight lines as opposed to crooked ones for instance – a house, a closet, a door or a picture frame will always have a straight top and bottom lines, or at least the left and right edges will be at the same height, levelled. A wall will always be flat surfaced. Like straight lines, patterns are preferred to non-patterns, and most of what we, humans, produce is based on patterns. Neither does Nature usually produce uneven, erratically arranged or unorganized forms. For example: a flower petal, a tree, the relatively flat surfaces of lakes and seas – these would have a beautiful wavy pattern to their motion, all have patterned forms. Even a big field of barley or wheat will grow to a similar height, (given that the plants had similar conditions under which to develop).

We all like to be around aesthetic or aesthetically made or arranged things. We will always prefer nice, good-looking things to not nice ones.

Femininity then is:

Humans' perception and interpretation of the most artistic and the most aesthetically possible way of being, living, moving, talking, reacting and thinking.

A feminine woman's motion is poetry, a human form of art.

Men's motion is more a practical one.

What does an aesthetic way of being, behaving mean?

When one examines motion, apparent motion, one finds that softer, smoother, gentler and more delicate motions are usually more aesthetic and closer to beauty. Quick and forceful motions can be impressive and beautiful as well, but not as beautiful. When you scream, talk roughly or move erratically, it is less agreeable than when you speak softly and nicely and move in a more harmonic way.

I believe that speed, roughness and sharpness represent pain and danger to us and, therefore, we mostly recoil from them. We mostly get hurt when something rough, sharp or aggressive happens, like a car accident, a fall, being struck by someone or something. These are all opposite motions to softness, delicacy and elegance. Even when we break up a relationship, or fight and argue, these are mostly done in harsh and aggressive ways with anger and resentment.

With regard to patterns, I guess we are, as a species, not able, at the moment, to handle too much information at once. We can get overwhelmed and confused when too much is happening; too much random motion or when faced with things or situations we are not familiar with. We'd like life to make sense and be essentially under our control. Perhaps that is why we've developed a fondness and preference for patterns and arranged forms, which we equate with order and things that can be easily processed by us mentally.

For motion to be created, energy is needed. One of the most basic units of energy – the power to move things, to create any kind of motion – is a wave. A wave is a flow of particles working together creating a pattern – all the sounds that we hear are types of energy, which come in different shapes and forms called waves or wavelengths.

For example, a wave of noise, which most of us can't really stand will look like this:

This next illustration of an energy wave is one of a nice and harmonic sound:

We can obviously see that the second one has a pattern, is smoother, nicer and more organized; has more grace.

Women, the gentler sex, the feminine gender, naturally and effortlessly adopt this type of motion to various degrees in almost everything they do. They, in comparison with men, move and go about doing things in a smoother manner and more elegantly; polished and with finesse. Their touch is usually warmer and more tender. Their smiles and facial expressions are softer and more delicate. Their tone of voice and the way they talk are generally more dulcet, and thus usually more pleasing to the ear. They are mostly graceful.

The way they touch, drive a car, eat, drink and just about anything they do is generally done in a softer, gentler way than men, in a more *harmonious motion*, thus more graceful and elegant. Most wear their hair long, giving their faces and appearance in general a boost of softness and elegance, like a regal horse with a long mane. Femininity then was naturally best to go to and be portrayed by the gentler sex, the less-masculine and life-giving gender; women.

Gentleness, softness and gracefulness, as mentioned, are part of femininity; hence, rough or sharp movements and gestures have been regarded as rude and unwomanly in most societies. Eating with your mouth open, for instance, is considered uncouth or bad-mannered in most cultures; women are more self-conscious about this and also generally about the way they eat in public or in company.

In the past, even the use of swear words in front of a lady was considered rude.

Furthermore, women normally react to just about anything less aggressively and more calmly, and are much less quarrelsome than men. Even the gazes women possess are softer and gentler than men's – gentleness is projected from within, it can then be detected in one's eyes – the reflection of one's perspectives and attitudes towards life. While men can project any type of quality, they don't normally project gentleness and softness. The relative calmness and gentleness of women, projected from within, help them remain generally more innocent than men – not naive, but innocent, specifically in their basic and initial set of responses and thought processes. This is discernible even when they smile; their smiles are more sincere and innocent than the average man's. When one is not biologically, psychologically and socially concerned, bothered or occupied with conquering and the urge for sex, one is able to generally be more innocent; honest, sincere and devoid of any thoughts or intentions unrelated to the matter or encounter at hand.

All of the above explains why a lady is treated with a certain respect; why humans conceived of and practice gentlemanliness and not ladyhood.

Also, the marvellous and very appealing fact that women can grow and bring new life in itself can induce gentlemanly conduct.

Due to all of the above:

Men and even women can be in awe of femininity. Femininity to men is like a life-full, beautiful landscape which, no matter how hard one tries to take it in, is still to an extent impossible to fully retain. Men's strong desire for women is primarily the desire for this different, admired, art-like quality.

Owing to one of the main distinctions between the sexes, that of being pursued as opposed to being the pursuer, women, who are used to being observed, looked and stared at, developed a set of reactions and 'no responses'. One of the natural, consequential patterns of behaviour or responses to when one is being admired or desired is to reply or respond humbly. When it comes to a woman being looked at, a common feminine response will be that soft, innocent and humble half look that they usually have or give when men look at them. That look is femininity itself; it comprises a big part of what femininity is. It says, I'm the pursued party, I know that, accept it and humbly and elegantly appreciate it. It is like a nod of appreciation or respect; it is a classy move.

None of which means that men comport and express themselves in an ugly manner, but simply that women usually do so more elegantly and gracefully; more harmoniously.

Femininity is a wavelength; which is, as said before, a manifestation of energy and motion. It is a wavelength of beauty and grace, one closely related to art.

Femininity is simply beauty, aesthetics; the notion of beauty.

Ultimately it is a perception of oneself – how one perceives one should be in the playground of life. This comes almost instinctively to women.

Men, traditionally and historically, have been more concerned with the physical part of life, the parts that require a little more strength and roughness.

Women also have slightly nicer and more aesthetic bodies. Their softer-looking faces, skin, hands and more rounded physique are partly responsible for that, but it is the quality of femininity that really makes the difference. They way women do things, walk, talk – their motion is graceful; they *project* more aesthetic, harmony and are therefore nicer to look at or simply are nicer looking. Hence, femininity is not necessarily and strictly an innate quality of women. They have inherited a biological composition that forged the basis for that quality and this, combined with the fundamental search for beauty and aesthetics by the human mind: the motion, quality, attitude and behaviour of what we call femininity, was perceived and created. Femininity thus is not genetically transferred from mother to daughter but is more a social consciousness and agreement that girls pretty much unconsciously embrace. This means that women have a choice in a way, and further, that when society's perceptions and agreements on the subject of femininity change, women's perceptions and concepts of it will also change. And indeed, perceptions and concepts with regards to femininity have been changing in recent decades. (We'll discuss this further in later chapters.)

Art is the highest form and endeavour for the human soul.

Art is creation and imagination. Although most people are not concerned with art or spend much time with it, nevertheless they have art and creation imprinted on their souls and, given the time, opportunity and some indoctrination, I suspect that the vast majority of people would choose to and try and engage in some capacity or another in art-related activities or forms of creation.

That might explain why, supported by biology, this way of being – femininity, the closest to art humans can be – was invented and embraced.

Art and aesthetics being the highest forms of life could, with some indoctrination and leadership, make society become increasingly aesthetics-oriented and improve life altogether. Art and aesthetics, in terms of everyday life and human behaviour, are expressed in the forms of femininity, grace, class, elegance and maturity in behaviour, composure, respect, dignity, cleanliness and civilized forms of communication with one another. I'm quite certain that all of us would want our society to be based upon these qualities and characteristics.

Grace

What is grace?

Grace comprises a big part of femininity and is closely related to beauty and aesthetics.

Grace is beauty and elegance in motion, action and fundamentally all interactions. *It is the art of motion.* It includes the way one reacts to things emotionally and verbally.

It feels and seems to me that very graceful people are quite aware of what it means to be graceful and are consciously in control over the way they are moving, doing things and interacting.

Whilst it's possible to encounter a graceful man, the term is usually reserved for women.

Women are naturally more inclined to grace, because they're naturally inclined to be feminine.

Gracefulness is also a mental trait. Though less noticeable and not as big an indicator as behaviour is, nevertheless, sincerity, intentions, ideas and integrity add or subtract plenty from the general way we perceive a person. Each of us is comprised of the sum of physical and mental attributes we possess and they're all being projected from within us. An astute person can perceive thoughts and intentions and have accordingly less or more appreciation for the person in question.

Being classy, what does it mean?

Well, the definition has been changing over time. Our concepts of and ideas on any subject can change with time and indeed, some aspects of behaviour which were regarded as classy a hundred years ago, are these days to a great extent considered too old-fashioned and redundant.

What do we mean by class? A classy man? A classy woman? A lady? Composure is one of the first things that springs to mind when I think of class. Not losing one's temper, handling things and matters dispassionately as much as one can, and in a relatively relaxed way without the need to resort to personal insults or attacks. For one to be genuinely composed one needs to truly have patience. Also, being compassionate and doing the right thing, even under impossible circumstances, all constitute class.

A classy person will be honest and sincere, will not lie. A dishonest person finds it almost impossible to conduct him/herself in a classy manner. Being composed and doing the right thing requires the belief and the conviction on the part of the person that he/she is doing the right thing. Furthermore, lying will, most of the time, be detected or eventually found out – or at least sensed. That will make a person untrustworthy and this is the opposite of class because class is considered to be a positive trait. Class is a mental state and the bedrock on which it stands is honesty.

The emotion of cursing is ugly. Words, however, are not the principle aggressor in swearing, they are much less dominant than the emotion which is being transmitted and directed at someone or something. When one curses he/she expresses resentment, hatred, anger; these are not waves (energy) of grace or beauty. While class does not necessarily mean grace, they are nonetheless very close to one another. A classy person would by definition have to conduct himself in a somewhat graceful manner. Composure, which is fundamental for class, is also one of the prerequisites for grace.

One of the highest concepts of 'class' is being oneself without attempting to be or act like another, nor having the intention to manipulate others or to elicit responses from them in ways other than through pure reason and logic. Pressing people's buttons or using any other manipulative methods to elicit a response in order to achieve something is not a true classy behaviour.

Why grace and class are important

The setting or backdrop to life: the sounds, sights and smells around us and of course people's behaviour, everything in our vicinity contributes to or detracts from our general sense of wellbeing and feeling. We feel better when we are well-dressed, clean and smelling good – well-groomed, in other words. A nice and elegant presentation of ourselves means class. Cleanliness is close to godliness: normally we all prefer to be in clean and tidy environments as opposed to messy and dirty ones. It makes us feel better. That is also why flight attendants behave gracefully and most official places dealing with the public attempt to be courteous, respectful and representable – which means basic class and grace.

On a behavioural level, when someone responds calmly and maturely to something we did or said and does not get upset at us even though it might have been merited, we appreciate that person and the way he/she reacted; it is heart-warming. When watching two people from the side (parents for instance) arguing in a respectful way, listening to one another and not losing their composure or temper, we look on in admiration and appreciation. When a man is being gentlemanly it's nice and aesthetic to the eye. It all adds to or improves the general atmosphere.

Being around crude people who argue, scream, shout and use profanities, as opposed to being near people who speak calmly and with respect makes a difference.

The mere reaction of someone to something can influence our moods for better or worse. The way one looks at us in response to something we've said or done, the way one replies verbally, the tone of voice she or he is using; each of these matters affects us to some extent. We are not fond of, and at the same time we're also sensitive to, ungraceful reactions, responses or behaviour.

Therefore, classy behaviour, comportment and surroundings can make a whole lot of difference to the quality of the lives we lead.

The ability to be classy and graceful is greatly influenced by social conditions, the times we live in and by random or particular circumstances. It's harder to control oneself, be composed and respectful, when one is constantly concerned with providing for oneself and one's family, when one is upset or offended or just weary of the daily routine and the mundane and tedious life one may feel one leads, as many of us do.

But it is still very possible, desirable and rewarding. Grace and class, being attitudes and approaches towards life, say a lot about a person and that person's perception of life and living. A classy person will feel better about himself and will be more appreciated and loved by others.

Grace and class come from within, obviously; they are states of mind.

When a woman is truly feminine she is better looking than when she is not. Her body and general looks are more appealing. If the same woman, with the same clothes, make-up and hair style, ceases to be feminine she will then instantly be less appealing and attractive.

Femininity and maturity

The older a woman gets the more feminine she is. One aspect of being feminine is maturity. This is an interesting thing. Feminine, graceful women, as discussed above, are calm; they react and respond in a refined manner, they express their negative emotions: anger, upset and the like –

if they do at all – in a lady-like, pacific manner. This is mostly a characteristic of maturity. Whether women were indoctrinated to behave so or otherwise does not change the fact that the result is a relatively mature comportment. They practice more self-restraint than men when it comes to reacting and expressing their emotions in public, or as quickly and as harshly as men can do. Women can obviously experience the same emotions and feelings as men but, due to all the reasons talked about so far in this book, women seem to be slightly less prone to even feel feelings such as aggression – much less express them in public. Women are also less quarrelsome as people. Being less inclined to feeling aggression, plus the ability to practice restraint, makes women more mature and sensible in the vast majority of cases.

Another boost of maturity

I've been noticing quite a remarkable thing that happens to girls/women when they turn twenty-seven to twenty-eight years of age. They seem to go through a second phase of maturity. Almost like a second puberty, only now uniquely on emotional and psychological levels. For some it happens earlier.

Although we can see the woman beginning to emerge from the girl as early as at the age of twenty or twenty-one, she nevertheless is still not fully a woman. Then, at twenty-seven or twenty-eight a transformation takes place. All of a sudden there is a more mature look in her eyes and an apparent deeper and better understanding of life and people. Women then become more feminine, sexier; more woman than girl. They become more self-conscious – for better or worse, more astute in general. They seem to be more focused, they seem to know more about what they want from life and from men. They have more composure in the company of men, but at the same time are more sensitive to them and more aware of men's general intentions. These changes rarely, if at all, happen to men.

We are all maturing day by day from the day we are born but both girls and boys go through a big transformative period on the physical and psychological levels when the libido appears at puberty. This process shoves them forward physically and mentally and provides them with more maturity, more awareness, sexual drive and a change of perspectives on life. The process of maturing continues on a psychological level in various degrees until we die.

We are all aware of the differences in maturity between women and men from a young age. Girls enter puberty, a process that lasts a few years, one year earlier, yet even two or three years later when both sexes are well into puberty, girls nonetheless have the advantage. It is not so much the fact that they start a year earlier as it is all the previously-mentioned biological and social reasoning which are responsible for the differences in maturity.

However, some men do mature as quickly and to the same level as women.

We can and indeed do keep maturing simply by going through life. We do so mainly at specific times and periods in our lives, after or during specific events and under some circumstances which can give us, both women and men, injections of maturity.

Still, women seem to stay ahead and maintain or increase that gap that had already formed in puberty. While most women's level of maturity continues to grow, many men seem to stop and stay still at some point in that regard.

Motherhood and fatherhood are two of the most specific maturing experiences for both women and men, but here as well, women normally make the bigger leap.

Women's infusion with maturity at twenty-seven to twenty-eight years of age seems to me to be the most influential natural occurrence for them, second only to puberty.

I can't say why this happens. But pay close attention if you will and see whether you notice the same changes within you or other girls/women you know. I find it to be a very interesting and appealing phenomenon.

Maturity means responsibility to a great extent. It seems that when a girl goes through puberty, a knowingness that she will have to be very responsible one day for one or more new human beings kicks in. Like a biological awareness moving up to the subconscious mind. By the same reasoning, biologically, when you have only one or a couple of chances a month to conceive and become pregnant – a matter of great importance to all living creatures – in comparison to giving millions of sperm cells each time you choose to do so, your perception of things in general will plausibly be different. You will be obliged to think things through and do so more thoroughly, not only in relation to sex, but possibly across the board. It appears very probable to me that this is one of the principal reasons why women are predominantly more responsible and mature people.

Thus, responsibility is one of the main elements of maturity. Should one wish to become more mature, taking responsibility will be the quickest way for that person to go about achieving it. Maturity is comprised of other elements as well, namely the ability to be empathetic, calm and composed. Practicing responsibility will greatly assist someone in eventually possessing these attributes as well.

Women have the advantage then; responsibility is in their core and they are 'officially' endowed with it at puberty, possibly even from birth – after all, it's in their biological blueprint. However, in the past the differences in maturity between men and women were less obvious, less accentuated. Life demanded more from a man, much more than it does today. Men had to be responsible for much more than they have been in recent decades. Generally, men had to be tougher; they very often faced harsh and difficult realities and situations. Greater necessity increases responsibility.

Femininity in the present

After inspecting what femininity is at its core, let us move ahead and review how this quality is faring at the present time.

Femininity of late has been eroding as a quality; very feminine women are almost like an endangered species. All of the beautiful things femininity means and represents are thus disappearing along with it.

There are possibly a few different explanations as to why this is occurring and why women are exhibiting less femininity at present than in the past, but, I believe the real and principal reasons for this phenomenon are the general decline in the *importance* of femininity as a concept and the way women regard femininity. Also, there is the lack of gentlemanliness and chivalry on the part of men of late, for which one of the main root causes is the self and social women-empowerment movements which have, in turn, been changing the expectations women have of men and the perceptions they have of life in general. It is no longer a world of ladies and gentlemen: "After all, if there are less and less gentlemen around then why try to be a lady? What for?"

People mostly adopt concepts and behavioural patterns from the people they come into contact with: parents, teachers, friends, etc; and from any type of information they may be exposed to. The chief culprits (at the least the chief collaborator and promoter) for the decline in the desire to be a feminine woman are the media. Most mediums of transference of information today are focused less on virtue and value and more on action, action figures and violence; anything that produces an impact and/or speed. The content they promote contains less class or classy behaviour and much less femininity.

Up until the 1950's in films and then on TV, drama and comedy were the focus. Actresses and actors were mostly graceful, had class and elegance, women were feminine, almost everything was done with patience and the contents of these programmes were much more modest than today's. 'Togetherness' was a prevalent concept. Moreover, the camera was either static, or moved relatively steadily. Soon after, slowly but surely, the industry began shifting towards more and more action-based movies, less and less conservative plots and depictions, less patience and grace, women increasingly became less feminine and more like men, camera movement started to be quicker and sharper, and pictures began to change much more rapidly (the antithesis of patience). Also, individualism had become almost more important than togetherness.

There are still many great drama and romance-based films being made today, but the bulk of films, TV series and especially music videos being created these days are largely not based on patience, elegance, class or values. Young people, who are plugged in in so many ways to media outlets and are constantly being bombarded by this kind of information, are no longer presented with many examples of real femininity, grace and virtue to draw upon.

There thus exists a decrease in the inclination and desire to be feminine, graceful or even aesthetic. Everything seems to be moving away from these concepts at present. A case in point: take a look at the way the average woman dresses today and compare that to the way women dressed in past generations. Also, the type of language many use at present. How did we move away from graciousness and the realization that profanities and bad language are neither classy nor graceful, to reach the point where cussing and using strong and sexual language is regarded as ok and even 'cool'? The way many women comport themselves at present is also testament to this aforementioned decline.

We've reached the point, in the 'modern'/western world, of almost disdain towards femininity. The term itself is on the verge of meaning old-fashioned or implying weakness; one that belongs to the ways of the past upon which many today look down. Oh boy, how quickly and drastically people can change!

A feminine, graceful woman is these days regarded as somewhat weak in the western world. A woman of a sort that represents the old times, when women were indeed feminine and graceful but also oppressed and considered inferior. The inability of women to distinguish between these two completely different things is very unfortunate.

Femininity is as far from weakness as muscles are from wits!

More on that subject is coming!

Romanticism

What is the percentage of people who are romantic, would you say?

Not too many, right?

Well, in my opinion most people, if not all, are born romantic, yes!

Imagine you open a business and fail. Then you open another one and fail again; assuming money is not a problem, you may consider opening a third one. But the third one happens to fail too. How do you think you'd feel? Would you try a fourth time? Probably not. Eventually you'd say to yourself, "I'm not cut out for that", or, "I have no luck, this is not for me, I'll go work in a corporation, work for someone else".

Let us make an analogy. Let's quantify your ability to be and remain optimistic and to preserve your belief in yourself. Suppose you have a pool of a hundred units of drive, motivation and vigour that you are endowed with at birth. Now, every time you fail, one, two, a few or even a dozen of these units are being transformed from their original state of vigour and belief into units of doubt, and are now filed in your memory as experiences that contain a failure, the feeling of failing or not succeeding. They also contain some bitterness, some regret and maybe sadness but, most importantly, doubt. These units are no longer at your disposal to be used as motivators or an incentive. The vigour in them is lost.

All of us go through numerous events in life that chip away at our pool of vigour, ambition and optimism. Some of us begin with a bigger pool of units of drive and belief than others and the blows we suffer during life don't completely knock us down. Some of us maintain an optimistic view even when we get knocked down and feel depleted. But we all, without exception, become less and less driven, optimistic and, I'm sad to say, cheerful, as we get older. No person is as happy at forty-five years of age as he/she used to be at five (except under the rarest circumstances). There are various reasons for this, yet one of the most significant ones is the failures we accumulate during our lives; not succeeding or achieving what we set out to achieve.

Hence, any person would have doubt in her/his heart and mind after she/he attempted to do or achieve things and failed (to various extents, the failures of the people around us influence us as well). Do you think it is any different with relationships? Failures in any aspect of life would manufacture fears, apprehensions and some distrust in ourselves with regard to the subject in which we failed, even though most won't realize or choose to accept the level and magnitude of these. Human interactions and relationships are a major and very basic part of our lives. That is why most of us keep trying to have and maintain a relationship despite everything. Alas, we do get more cynical, bitter and distrustful with each time we fail. (Cynicism: the belief that people do things solely to further their own individual interests coupled with the disbelief that people or life in general are fair, good and honest)

Each new relationship we begin will generally have a smaller chance of being realized the way we originally dreamt of it. Romanticism means strong connection, love, dedication and devotion. We usually give it all when we first fall in love, we put a big effort to make the relationship work, we fully believe it can. But when it doesn't, it knocks some of the wind out of our sails. Some people dream of true love, some of a good, sincere and practical relationship. But regardless of what each of us envisaged when young and innocent, we all become less convinced that it will actually be realized the more we fail at it.

Yet we must go on, life goes on and there is nothing we can do about the past. We try to start anew, fresh, to make the next relationship work and not to dwell too much on past relationships. Still, many things from our yesterdays are imprinted on our minds (regardless of how convinced one can be that the past doesn't influence one), mainly what should be the most obvious, but what usually gets the least amount of due attention, namely, the simple fact that we set out to succeed but failed; we didn't make the last or the last few relationships work. Other matters habitually resonate more with us: the fights, the disagreements, the break-up or anything else that made us feel bad or hurt.

Generally we are, at present, more cynical than people from previous generations. This trend has been going hand in hand with the increase in manipulation, greed and the 'take-care-of-number-one' culture that exists today. This kind of culture has emerged not necessarily because people today are different and less honest in their core but due to the increase in media and communications outlets over the last hundred years, their ever-increasing reach and the contents they promote. These outlets, the prime, and for most the only, source of information and entertainment, have been pushing and spreading more negative news and stories than positive ones, making us believe there is more evil than good in the world, more dishonesty than honesty, more infidelity than fidelity. This has been creating fear, apprehension and distrust. The results can be seen in the introverted and individuated people we are today; the 'take-care-of-number-one' culture.

Due to this ever more cynical culture, among other reasons, people today are increasingly engaged in short-term relationships principally based on sex, or just for the fun of it. When one does so, one actually practices the opposite to being romantic. This further erodes one's self belief in romanticism. In such an environment many will lose their romantic convictions and expectations *long* before turning into adults, without even having the chance to go through a few failed relationships or heartbreaks.

I'm of the opinion that people are born romantic but get corrupted with time. Romanticism is a very fragile quality and ideal. Like many a concept the mind holds, it is very easy to break, spoil or distort.

Objects of desire

Since I was a child I have been intrigued by the concept of falling in love. It has always been an inseparable part of my life; the search for the woman who will fill a void in me, a void I believe all of us have. Traditionally as well as today, men are those charged with the duty of courtship and pursuit in the race to fill that void. Most women are aware of that from a young age; aware of the great interest boys have and show in them. Some sense that interest constantly. To be wanted, desired, sought-after is very pleasing and confidence-building but it has its disadvantages too.

Young women, especially those who become habituated to constant attention, can turn vain, and therefore rather removed. This is understandable and justified to an extent when every other boy or a man stares at you on the street, at the cafe, in the shop or any other possible place. The lives of pretty girls and women are a little different from those of the rest of us. Men, by salivating over every good-looking woman they see are greatly at fault for that condition.

This can be really destructive to a girl/woman who has always been pretty or beautiful and has had that kind of attention from an early age. When one is being looked at all the time, chased after, pursued and desired primarily because of or for one's looks, one's perspectives on things and life are often shaped accordingly, and will differ from someone who is treated chiefly as a person rather than a pretty face. One's behaviour will most likely also change. One way in which this is evident to us is the growing number of pretty women and men who maintain something of a snobbish attitude because they know they are good-looking. Only in a society fixated on looks can such an attitude exist.

Taking everything into account, getting all that attention is not necessarily a positive thing then. It impels these girls and women to focus more on being pretty than just simply being. It compels them to view life through the eyes of their suitors, through a perspective that places more importance on looks rather than on character and substance, and to some degree or another forces them to conclude that people in general care more about looks than substance. This will most likely sadden a smart and profound girl/woman who is looking for substance and would like to be taken and viewed accordingly.

Men's pursuit of women is on a whole other level when compared to women's pursuit of men. Men drool over women while women are far more composed, calm and collected when it comes to the pursuit of and the viewing of men. Women usually go as far as "oh, he's cute, sexy, he has a nice a..." Of course, there are exceptions and some women, in particularly these days, are much racier and more direct. Nonetheless, most women, in practice and on a psychological level, are never completely consumed with chasing the opposite sex and, thankfully, looks are *still* not the primary concern of most women.

Society has increasingly become looks-oriented and less character-oriented in recent decades. When a culture idolizes good-looking women and men and – because of their looks – gives them much, much more coverage and attention than a person who is a humanitarian, for instance, or to stories of good deeds and goodness... well, you get the picture.

Magnifying glass

I've been observing an interesting, common phenomenon in most relationships between men and women. There seems to be a constant need and attempt on the part of men, as small as it may be, to keep women satisfied. Women generally do things more responsibly, more honestly and more for the sake and betterment of all parties involved (women are more socially conscious and normally hold to higher standards). Consequently, men are always under some suspicion, under scrutiny, always under a magnifying glass, if you will. Men are aware of this: while some never utter a word about it, others rue that reality and complain that their women expect too much of them.

On the other hand, men hold women in high regard and have great expectations of them. Often a man can get upset, angry or jealous because his woman or a woman has done something which was below the standards we, men or society hold them to: being ethical, pure, graceful, beautiful. When that happens I feel that men, unawares, believe they are losing a little of their grip on the one thread left holding everything which is pure and decent together in this world: *women.* It is man's subconscious quest to have and hold some semblance of purity and beauty in this world, a world men know at first hand is far from perfect.

Think about it… why would a man call a woman a slut? Why would men think like that when a woman sleeps around or is 'easy'? Nobody calls a man a slut for sleeping with many women. Of course, there is ignorance, prejudice and simple social patterns, repetition and imitation, but I believe that men's quest for purity is the more elemental and more profound rationale for why they react and act in this way.

Due to woman's biological composition; her ability to grow and bring life – being almost the sole guardian of future generations, her body being the one penetrated, her being the pursued and courted gender and all of her beautiful aforementioned feminine qualities – she is therefore held in the highest regard by men and women alike. She is considered as wholesome as a human being can be. She is expected then to comport, behave and take care of herself with more dignity and restraint. Men often react more violently to seeing a woman behaving in an unvirtuous way than to most other social and cultural infringements. Men, knowing in the back of their minds that they are not as pure as women, are consciously but predominantly subconsciously anxious for women to remain pure and virtuous. This is because most men *wrongly* suppose that they are unable to ever be as wholesome as women and that the only thing that can be or maintain a semblance of purity in their lives – in this impure and imperfect world – is women. It is almost men's last remaining chance, knowing themselves and their urges and drives, to live with or be around something relatively innocent and unspoiled.

That is one of the reasons why when women cheat on their men it is, and always has been, frowned upon much more severely than when men cheat (excluding the western world of late). Women are supposed to be pure. It really maddens men when women cheat, it is unbearable to most men. I believe that this is mostly because of the reasons mentioned above.

This concept, of women being held in higher regard, was apparently common knowledge in the past. Most women understood their role in keeping at least a little sense of ethics and purity in society. Most used to take pride in that.

Many of the restrictions placed on women's bearing, speech and behaviour throughout history were predominantly conceived because many of the behavioural patterns, ways of expression and comportment which were normal for men were considered for women – those who are held in higher regard – to be unfeminine, un-ladylike. Whether it was certain gestures, the way one speaks, the things one says, comportment or dress code; and let's not forget sex, either.

Men have always taken pride in being near or with a woman who was feminine, aesthetic, classy and graceful. There were not many other things which made men prouder. It seems like most people in the past believed that for the sake of society, women should be feminine and ladylike.

Calming influence

I grew up in Israel in a nice neighbourhood, attended school near my home and high schools in nearby cities. Spending most of my time outdoors with and among others, I got to know many people and had constant contact with them. Some young men had a rough demeanour about them. Altercations, fist fights and mischief were neither a rarity nor a surprising thing in my neck of the woods. But one particular thing was to me always intriguing and heartwarming, and that was seeing the calming influence a woman would generally have on enraged or hot-tempered boys and men. Very often a provoked, angry, furious, violent or aggressive guy would instantly become less so when his girl, or a girl, came on the scene. These boys would generally become less prone to altercations when their girlfriends were present. It is as if feminine-related qualities, like gentleness and softness, could dispel some of the man's aggression. At the same time, it could have been the command she had on him – it's quite remarkable to see how strong and independent men listen to the wisdom of the woman by their side. Seemingly, we men know that a woman's internal wisdom is more profound than ours and that women are more sensible and hold higher standards of behaviour. Men know that in the vast majority of situations a woman would seek a logical and pacific solution and would try to avoid a violent confrontation or altercation. Men are generally calmer and more relaxed having a woman in their lives.

As a side note: this book mostly glorifies women and at the same time does not speak very highly of men. This does not mean that men are not such good people as women in their core, nor that they are incapable of being so. Nor does it mean that men can't have all the great qualities women normally possess. Men potentially are and can. This book simply lays out some of the reasons and reasoning behind why they still aren't and why it is harder for them to be so.

Sex

Sex is an urge and a desire we all share, and a strong one too. Why?

I can think of three reasons why sex would be such a powerful impulse. The first one will be the biological factor. Let's look at it more closely. A body is just like a machine, it has no real awareness. Bodies are biologically programmed to develop the necessary bodily substances and functions for reproducing and procreating, to create more bodies in order to perpetuate their specie. We all develop a libido at a young age. It is in our genetic codes. A big part of the impulse to have sex is this underlying compulsion and addiction to the act of procreation, perpetuation. That is why evolution placed so many sense and pleasure receptors in our genitals. That is why the brain interprets these signals to mean great pleasure. Biological needs can be very demanding. Think of times when you were really hungry, for instance, when your body demanded to be fed, remember how difficult to concentrate or even to think it was? Some urges or biological needs create stress in us, physical as well as mental. However, when it comes to sex, unlike hunger that will eventually kill us, the control, decision and choice to accommodate that urge are still in our hands, in us; in the aware part of us, the person her/himself.

The second factor: Many people believe that they are more than just a body; that they are a spirit or that they have a soul. Accordingly, they hope or believe (many more did in the past) that when we die we come back and start anew in another body. I'm of the opinion that we all, as thinking and aware people, subconsciously share some small hidden hope or belief or possibly even knowingness that this may be true, and therefore there exists in us an underlying need and desire to perpetuate life through the creation of new bodies, so we have a way to live again. Hence the mental/spiritual urge for sex and procreation. Were this to be true, the older one gets the more anxious one would be with regards to sex. Anxiety *does not* suggest more sexual vigour and desire though.

The third reason why sex is such a central theme in our lives is proximity, closeness.

On a psychological, mental or spiritual level, the closer you are to another, the more affinity you will have for that person. That is a law in this world, from humans all the way through to the smallest particle. All things and living creatures strive for proximity.

Having sex is in actuality the closest you can be to another human being (apart from being in your mother's womb – no wonder the mother-child bond is so strong). In sex we are not just close, we are joined together to some extent, inside one another. The most intimate a couple can get is when they are making love.

Another very good example of the importance and impact proximity has on us would be a hug. Think of a big, warm, tight hug; it can really generate powerful emotions.

On a side note, people who appreciate hugs, (innocent hugging, not for the purpose of making out) are more romantic and warmer people. Most women are naturally aware of that and sense that instantly. (I thought I'd mention that as a tip for getting to know someone or to figure her/him out, in case you did not already know that.)

A word about the enjoyment of sex

There are numerous factors contributing to or detracting from the enjoyment of sex. I'd like to point out two key factors, though: first, obviously, the level of attraction you feel to your partner for which many things can contribute or detract from; second, the level of enjoyment and satisfaction of your partner – the more your partner enjoys the more arousing and enjoyable it will be for you and the more satisfying the act.

Normally, the overall and actual quality and enjoyment of sex depend greatly on the performance of the man. Men are much easier to please. Women are much more complex and require deeper attention and knowhow on the part of the man. Besides, women are different from one another, they enjoy different things, done in different ways. Men need to be open, observant, patient and willing to learn and change in order to be really good lovers.

Cynicism, a disease

What does cynicism have to do with femininity and relationships? What really is cynicism?

Cynicism is a metastasizing mental and emotional cancer.

Let's say you, as a woman, were hurt by men on five or six different occasions – cheated on, lied to, betrayed. You also happen to know of similar experiences your friends had. The foregone conclusion you and most women will likely reach is that it is very unlikely you will be able to find a good and honest man with whom you could have a long and lasting relationship, like your parents or your grandparents had. You will to an extent become a cynic (just as a reminder, cynicism is the belief that people do things to solely further their own individual interests coupled with the disbelief that people or life in general are fair, good and honest).

But is this real? True? Accurate? Getting hurt several times is certainly a lot, and is enough to render someone something of a nonbeliever. Yet objectively, this is an incorrect conclusion to draw and it's partly an emotional response to the circumstances. A single woman does not date a thousand men, and she probably doesn't know enough women who have together accumulated dates with thousands of men to make an empirical and scientific statement on the subject. Even when this 'fact' keeps being repeated by people on TV, in movies and even by prominent figures, it still doesn't make it true.

However, most of us reach a point where it is easier to give up and give in than to keep believing or stay optimistic and positive; the hardest tasks a grownup person faces are those in relation to one's personal dreams, goals and very much with regard to one's relationships. Were we able to keep an objective eye and analyse things dispassionately, we would most likely reach the conclusion that it is very plausible that there are good and honest men out there – they do exist. There are numerous stories of happy couples and successful relationships if we care to look and observe more closely.

More importantly, even if the chances of finding more than a handful of honest people are slim, it is still much more conducive to our mental health and lives in general to remain optimistic and believe in the goodness of people and in the possibility of finding true love or the right person. The alternative would be to become a non-believer, a cynic. But cynicism is a slow death. It will make one sick emotionally and possibly physically, too. Optimism and positivity are life itself. They will keep you going, they will give you strength. Even when we've just been hurt again and it's very painful and hard to collect ourselves, to pick up the pieces and to remain cheerful, we'd better view and recognize this pain, that difficult period, for what it is: a specific occurrence or person that hurt us, or a relationship that went wrong. Even if it's the fourth or fifth incident in a row, it still doesn't mean that each and every person in the whole world is like that. We'd best try and put it behind us and look forward with the belief that the next relationship could be a great one. This is extremely difficult to do. Yet it is still possible to hold on to these optimistic perspectives and to distinguish the pain from the objective knowledge that good and honest people do exist. It is possible to be aware of disturbing information based on some observations – for instance, that snakes are perilous to humans – but at the same time to find many, through objective and composed inspection, that aren't.

Most of us naturally become a little more cynical each time we get hurt or after our trust has been broken. Yet, developing an attitude which is mainly composed of lack of optimism, even if we do go on and start a new relationship, will reduce our chances of success in the future. Cynicism is a condition, one which exhibits symptoms on mental, emotional and physical levels. No person who has a tumour growing inside is in great shape. You must be thinking: "That's easier said than done!" You're right, it is hard; still, it's possible! Let's assume that by taking this difficult path and adhering to my recommendations you will remain a mere ten percent more optimistic than you would have been otherwise. This would mean ten percent happier, more contented or conversely less despondent. It means you'll have ten percent more chance of finding the right person. Any improvement in our quality of life is more than welcome. Belief and optimism can certainly provide us with that improvement.

There is an even quicker way in which we can become cynical, and that is to hurt another, to act immorally, break trust or do anything that we wouldn't like done to us. Doing deeds of this kind is even more detrimental to us than when the same is done to us. When we do things we know are not ok, just, fair or moral we actually force our own perspectives to change with regards to those things and with regards to life in general. For example, when we cheat, our perspectives on the subject of cheating will change; we now believe that people can cheat; we did this, cheated, therefore others must be capable of doing it as well. We normally assume that if we are capable of something, others are too. The closest living creature to you is you and the closest and most accessible knowledge about people and interactions is inside of you; your own experience. Therefore, when a person lies frequently, he/she will trust no one. That person 'knows' at first hand that people have the capability to and do lie. When a man flirts with other women when he is drunk he will suspect his wife of doing the same after she has had a few drinks. That is mainly why more men than women are jealous people. At least that is the way it used to be. The more women act irresponsibly and immorally with regard to relationships, the more jealous they'll become.

Hence, doing things which you know are not ok and that you shouldn't do will very rapidly distort your viewpoints, ideals and beliefs and will render you more and more cynical.

Why do you suppose children are so happy and positive? One reason and one reason only: optimism, zero cynicism! Children do not view people as potential cheaters, liars and offenders nor do they knowingly hurt another. They are innocent. Innocence is a very precious attribute that is eroded and taken away from us little by little each time we fail, get hurt, offended, lied to, cheated on or, conversely, when we knowingly do these things to others.

Women at present

When a time comes when whispers for change become loud voices and enough people create a force which can no longer be repelled or suppressed, a change or a shift in cultures and societies occurs. We then get the opportunity to change an inequality, an unfavourable state of affairs or a long-lasting injustice. We commonly go about this by changing old rules, writing new laws and also by adjusting our social attitudes, mores and opinions. But at times we can also take these a few steps too far. We try really hard to detach ourselves from the old ways of the near or distant past and we sometimes also, to a greater or lesser extent, part from good sense and logic. The simple reason for this is that, when finally given the opportunity to change and make things better, we jump head-first into the task and quickly attempt to alter and forsake the bad and currently frowned-upon ways of the past. Consequently, without much contemplation, or at least real objective contemplation, we go to some extremes and do everything pretty much opposite to what had hitherto been the status quo. All we can see and think about is how to put those old and dark times behind us. Instead of remaining calm, composed and rational, we, full of emotions, sprint to embrace an opposite approach and set of beliefs. Feminism is to some degree an example of that.

The first wave of feminism was extremely important. From time immemorial until recently, the opinions about and with regards to women were ridiculous and ignorant. Women were considered inferior to men in most countries and cultures and in most eras of life.

Honestly, I cannot understand how men could have considered such beautiful and remarkable creatures to be inferior. Nevertheless, that was the case. Hence something had to be done, something had to change. And it did. In the late 19th century and at the beginning of the 20th century things began to take a turn for the better. Women were being granted equal rights in most fields, many reforms were passed and things looked to be in the ascendant. Gender-based inequality was fading away. There was a lot more to be done, of course, but the stage was set and wheels were in motion; the world was changing for the better. More progress was made in the following decades.

But the quest for equality and forsaking of the discriminatory past has wrongly driven many women to seek a complete equality with men, not only with respect to rights, but also on physical and emotional levels. Recently, many women in western societies have been attempting to be more like men. There seems to exist an unspoken tendency in today's world to become less womanly, whether this is done consciously or otherwise. This can be seen in a growing number of women by their comportment (many have found a middle-of-the-road way of comporting themselves – unlike a man but not very feminine either; even their gaze is less feminine: body movement, speech and gaze are all manifestations of one's attitudes and perceptions). Some have started to use men's jargon, men's gestures and jokes and some even try to be as crude as some men are: getting drunk or speaking and behaving in coarse and vulgar ways. All of the above is done to various degrees depending on how much the woman is trying to forsake her femininity. Most have chosen a middle ground.

Nevertheless, a huge number of women have forsaken femininity, in the classic and traditional sense, to some extent or another. They have done so because they are under the impression that being and acting less feminine and womanly and more like men is better, tougher, more cool and that it makes them equal. The "Men do that, behave like so, are allowed this and that, then so do we and so will we" kind of attitude. In a way it is more 'cool' to not give a damn and be rough than to be gracious, delicate and feminine in their minds. A large number of these women attempt to embrace the 'freedoms' men traditionally have had. The freedoms to not care much about the way one looks, talks, the things one says and the way one behaves. Men in the past rarely felt or were held accountable for their behaviour, the things they said or for the way they said them. I feel that women today would also like, to a degree, to be free of self and public scrutiny and from ethics and social mores – another reason why women are becoming less feminine, graceful or classy. In addition, having not had control over their lives and livelihood, being very often controlled and treated as an inferior gender physically and in terms of rights and opportunities, many women today enjoy feeling and being on the other side of that equation, the side that is in control and the good feelings that come with it – whether it be the positivity of simply being free to be and express yourself or the ego-feeding part of it; the being in-charge, in control – this can be addictive to one degree or another for many people.

Due to this new outlook of equality, femininity has also come to mean weakness. Many women believe that when a woman is feminine she can't do or achieve what men can. In addition, there is that knowledge in the backs of their minds that in the past when women were more feminine, the world was chauvinist and patriarchal, meaning they were considered to be inferior conceptually and practically, often being taken advantage of – like when men could molest or harass women and get away with it or simply patronize them, treat them badly or discriminate against them. Thus, quite a lot of women in various countries around the world are trying to lose that gentle, delicate look and begin to speak and act tough like a man, or simply in ways they believe are different to looking fragile and weak or projecting weakness; they don't want to be treated like a weak person or to be patronized. This is obviously understandable: it's definitely not easy being a woman in a man's world. Some women even fear looking or appearing fetching because men might view them as a sex object and thus not take them seriously, or will hire them simply because of the sexuality they project or to potentially have an affair with them. I say, first, a feminine, womanly and aesthetic woman does not mean weakness and fragility. And when a woman has class, it is class that's being projected and not sexuality, no matter how fetching she might look. But even when a woman is just a girl and her boss or manager perceives her predominantly as a sex object, that's his problem. These days men can't act on their desires and wants like in the past; women are pretty much safe. They do not need to hide their womanly features anymore. If someone hires me and views me as anything other than my real self, so be it. I'll do my job, be myself and things will eventually fall into place.

These changes to the way women view and regard femininity in recent times have been happening because women wrongly believe or have forgotten that their innate qualities are more precious than men's and to be like men is not necessarily a move up, *on the contrary*. Feminine-related qualities are being pushed to the margins while lower-level 'qualities' are being sought after and admired. To be 'cool', for instance, is an attribute favoured over gracefulness in our current times. More on that later on.

The invention of mass media platforms made it possible and easy to reach each and every one of us, and to influence and manipulate people on a grand scale. It is not at all difficult to manipulate the minds of people – it can simply be done by pressing their buttons sufficiently, especially when they relate to sex. Sex is a touchy enough subject, let alone when it is being pressed and triggered continuously by the content on TV, in movies, music and on the internet. It becomes even easier again when society is looking to move away from the ways of the past, which advocated the suppression of sex and sexual needs, the prohibition of the expression of sexuality in public and the former expectation of women to remain virgin until their wedding night. All of the above have brought about the increasingly opposing and opposite approaches with reference to sex that we are witnessing today, and which have gone way too far in my opinion (and that of many others too, as far as I can gather).

The degree to which sex was suppressed in some cultures and religions in the past was large. At times the individual was made to feel guilty just thinking about it. Yet people of past generations knew something for a fact that many of us have forgotten. The minute you open the door to and willingly submit, or give in, to sexual urges you're asking for trouble on a grand scale.

Betrayals, infidelity, lies, plenty of divorces and break-ups have their roots in sexual wants and desires.

We *do* occasionally stray too far to the other side when looking for a change. For many women, equal rights came to mean everything is acceptable, all is ok; if men can do it so can they, if men are allowed to so should they. That is not utterly incorrect. It is obviously true concerning many facets of life. However, following in the footsteps of men in subjects like sex and relationships is very ill-advised. After all, all women – and many men as well – know and have always known that men's behaviour can be often bad, demeaning, discriminatory, animalistic and hurtful concerning these subjects. Every woman knows how fleeting, nonspecific and pervasive men's sexual wants are. For thousands of years women generally resented that. We all used to agree and still do that cheating on your spouse is a horrible thing. Having sex with many women is immature. Being guided or controlled to an extent by urges, especially the urge and need for sex that make men unable to think straight, has always been considered a weakness. Women bemoaned these attitudes and behaviour of men for centuries upon centuries and then, just like that, one sunny decade or a few ago, a big chunk of western society's female congregation seemed to have forgotten most of that and began to adopt the ways and behavioural patterns of men.

The ramifications of these changes in attitudes do not paint a lovely picture. At present, more and more men and women, both genders, behave irresponsibly, without virtue and carelessly with regards to sex and relationships. These translate to less marriages, less lifelong relationships, more broken homes, more individuation, introversion and generally more misery.

Women who have adopted that philosophy are in actuality *lowering* themselves to the level of men. Instead of controlling the fire and perhaps letting it subside they are adding more fuel to it. This is the equality women have been striving for? In what way this is productive or wise?

Women, the more wholesome gender, should demand that men – like they used to – climb up to their level, to be better, more responsible, more truthful, less animalistic and not lower themselves to the level of men by thinking that by being free to do and behave in that way they are more equal. A woman who used to be loyal and monogamous, but then begins to cheat and have occasional sexual encounters or partners has practically and objectively stooped to a lower level.

Women used to be exemplars of the better and more sensible side of humanity – they largely still are. But were we to continue in the direction society has taken of late, we may soon enough not have anyone to look up to. The degree to which society accepts or doesn't accept something has a great influence on people's minds and behaviour patterns. Thus, if we were to carry on and accept this decline in values, people and cultures will decline even further. Women, generally, as a gender have been for ages a source of inspiration and role models in many respects and especially with regards to sex and relationships. Were we to lose that then who will there be to set an example? Who will remind us vocally or tacitly about the kind of spouses we should be? Who will make us want to be better people?

Independence

Most women in the western world these days consider themselves independent. They are too, to various degrees of course but still much more so than in the past. This is mostly a good thing. This modern-day phenomenon is a result of the social and cultural changes that have been occurring over the last hundred years or so. Women have been increasingly able to get work, have their own careers, express their opinions, their tastes and have a choice in life and marriages, inevitably making them more independent in mind and body. Furthermore, given the nature of the relationship and connection between mother and child, women are the ones who are predominantly entrusted with the raising of offspring. This makes financial independence an even more important subject for women in a day and age where marriages break up like twigs on a bonfire.

But, when a woman sets on her way to becoming independent, economically or otherwise, her state of mind to a greater or lesser extent then changes and moves away from the "we share everything", or "we're together for life" attitudes of the past and increasingly toward the "it's all up to me and me alone" attitude that's prevalent in society today – and justified to a degree.

Supposing two people share a common desire to be and stay together, their level of intimacy and the basic decision to stay together come rain or come shine, or the motivation to work hard when obstacles present themselves and their ability to keep it all together, all would suffer a blow when one or both of them are in "I am independent" mode. This will reduce the quality of the togetherness of the couple and the family. There is a very fine line we have to walk in order to both be independent and also to have a strong and sound togetherness.

Togetherness is a concept, an idea we need to hold on to, and like any concept or idea its importance can be eroded and annulled all together. Being alone is also a concept, one which is much easier to resort to than to hold on firmly to the concept of 'togetherness'. A person to a degree is always alone in her/his body and her/his mind. Therefore, this idea (being alone) in comparison to 'togetherness' is much easier to slip or slide back into while 'togetherness' requires more effort to keep.

When one puts a lot of stress on independence one inevitably projects it and this can also be detected in one's attitudes and actions. A person can indeed feel that she/he is able to live on her/his own and that they do not necessarily need anyone. That can very well be true. Yet 'alone' is not the most beneficial and productive way for us to be and live. These attitudes of independence are at present being reflected in the manner and speed at which couples break up and decide to let the relationship and/or the family dissolve. It's manifested in the reduced level of compromise between couples, too, and in the reduced effort they expend in order to keep the relationship going. This sense of independence can and often does obscure a person's ability to appreciate or simply to 'forget' the value of the-two, of the family or the relationship.

The majority of men have been disloyal all through history. Yet they would almost never break up the family and marriage if they could help it. Primarily because of their fear and inability to be alone, but also because they knew and appreciated the value of having a person to lean on and build and maintain a family with. This independence-phenomenon of late is heavily backed by, and to a great extent the result of, the 'take-care-of-number-one' culture we have today.

Here too, women have gone a little bit too far to the other side. They have moved from being mostly 'effect' with regards to independence to being too much 'cause'". They are not to blame of course, we all simply try to adapt to new realities and circumstances the best way we can. Women as a gender could most probably survive alone better than men if push came to shove. Still, we must not stray too far with 'independence'. Women should not push men aside too much. Women should not wage a vendetta against men and the past. They are sensible enough to know and do better.

Women! You often forget and perhaps do not fully realize the power and advantages you have over men given to you innately – the power to be pregnant, bear children, motherhood and the relative peace of mind and feeling of contentment you inherit or are endowed with. All making you more able to bear life and its loneliness. The level of your potential contribution to a family, life and the world in general is grand. Men are aware of this – consciously but largely subconsciously – and are constantly being reminded of that by simply sharing a life with a woman and/or having a family. Therefore, as said earlier we men need to do a lot in order to merely come close to contributing as much as you do to the family, and to life in general. It is extremely hard for men to close the gaps on these advantages women possess. Many women, by becoming independent and by perhaps attempting to prove they can do it all on their own, whether it be with regard to financial matters or simple tasks at home or in the family, are of late introducing an additional problem and obstacle for men to overcome. In doing so, they overlook the detrimental effects and ramifications this has on men and in turn *on them.*

I believe that, deep down inside, most women would like their men to be strong and to contribute at least as much as they do to the relationship and/or the family, as well as believing in and practicing togetherness! Yet, this ideal scenario is getting increasingly tougher to realize due to all of the women-empowerment programmes, policies and trends we are recently seeing in schools, universities and places of work, and therefore also inside women's minds and in their homes.

Women! Let men be men, let them make some decisions and take some responsibility. Don't eliminate what's left for them to contribute to or be 'cause' over. Let them do some man stuff and feel needed; they surely need you! This doesn't mean you shouldn't take a job, have a career or be able to sustain yourself financially. Societies and the world will benefit from well-balanced and complementary relationships.

Relationships and sex today

Most men and women at present in the western world will have had a few or more relationships by the time they get married, if they do at all. Many these days are under the impression that more is good. They would argue that to have different partners is interesting, refreshing and experience-building, and thus assists them in finding the best or the right person or being generally able to choose a partner more wisely.

I feel that most women, at heart, would still like to find the one person, fairly early in their lives, and stay with that person. Yet, it is getting increasingly tough for women not to become part of this trend, having a few or more relationships before settling on the one. This has penetrated society deeply and become accepted and normal. In addition, the difficulty in maintaining a relationship for long these days can only contribute to this trend.

Another thing that has been introduced into our culture in recent decades is the notion that dating a couple or a few guys/girls at the same time is ok and a normal thing. Men do this more of course, but women are catching up. Both sexes justify this behaviour by saying to themselves that it's a numbers game and when there is more than one good prospect at the same time you don't pass on the opportunity to check it out. Also, doing this at the beginning of a relationship is ok; it's considered still to be the dating phase with no real commitment given yet. Clearly none of us would like to be treated that way; be dating someone and to find out that she/he is dating someone else concurrently. Yet we seem to care less about the feelings of the other of late, hence the justifications.

The times in which we're living and the changes we are experiencing can be indeed confusing to both women and men but throwing reason, empathy and mores to the wind is not the solution.

Were society to have a moral back-bone on which we all could lean and be guided by, we could all then do better and remain more principled. But in these last decades society's emphasis on values like loyalty and fidelity has been diminishing. When there is no real expectation of people being virtuous (not letting external influences or feelings and wants control you and dictate your behaviour, but doing the right thing by you and the people around you), the outcome will be people who are increasingly giving in to their inner urges and desires.

A growing number of women currently believe that having occasional sex or having many sex partners and therefore concentrating less on a serious relationship, or simply putting it on hold, make them equal to men in that regard. "Why is it socially 'accepted' for men and not for women?" They would also justify it by arguing what has become a prevalent argument in western society today; an argument that supports the satisfaction of one's sexual needs without much regard for the consequences. "I'm human", "I have needs". Some women would still, on principle, resent the way many men use women only for sex but at the same time embrace a similar approach and 'use' men for the very same thing. These changes in attitudes in an increasing number of women play into the hands of men looking for sex and thrills. Instead of enforcing more ethical behaviour in men, these allow them to act even more immorally and irresponsibly.

That kind of short-term thinking and the rather destructive viewpoints with regard to relationships and sex came about as a result of almost a century of a care-of-the-body culture emerging alongside the reforms which gave rise to equal rights, opportunity and freedoms to women in many countries around the world. A care-of-the-body culture means the placement of greater emphasis and importance on the body and attending more to one's bodily needs, urges and frailties than to one's virtues and character.

The last century has brought us to the verge of almost the complete introversion and individuation of people; the thinking of oneself primarily and solely. The roots of these phenomena can be chiefly tracked back to some ridiculous theories that originated in central Europe. These proclaimed that humans have no souls and that they are composed of only matter or chemicals; having people believe that their body is all they have, all that they are. When a person 'knows' she/he is going to die and there is nothing after death and that she/he is nothing more than a perishable body, that person becomes more anxious to satisfy her/his short, and possibly meaningless life as much as she/he can.

Ideas and concepts become truths in people's minds when there is no one or nothing to show or prove them otherwise. Given the metaphysical nature of the soul, it was fairly easy for people to begin to question the existence of it when presented with new 'scientific' data. These modern theories then gain traction and gave rise to concepts like: 'you only live once', 'looking-out-for-number-one', and then, 'why give myself to one woman/man?' 'Why not lie and steal, do drugs, get drunk?' etc… These are concepts and ideas that, granted, have always been around but undoubtedly have become more prevalent in recent times.

Soon after the inception of these theories, taking care of the body became a prime concern for people. And what is more matter and chemistry than to eat, drink, care about one's looks and have sex?

Alas, the more we tend to the body the more we need to tend to it. As a consequence, the body becomes our everything, all to be concerned about. Obsession of the body culture had begun.

From that point onward, the road to bodybuilding competitions and beauty pageants was short and smoothly paved.

Before too long, one could sell anything under the sun if it held the promise of making one look better or feel better about his/her physicality, and thus about his/herself.

Curiously enough, the importance invested in the body in ages past was more considerable, but in a very different way! Most people believed in the existence of the soul, in virtue and substance and that they were NOT the body. The body was considered merely a vessel for the soul, for the person. There used to exist a term in the past, 'the sanctity of the body'. Originating in religion, it nevertheless was a concept embraced by most. It basically meant control over one's bodily urges; using one's body with dignity. I do not mean to suggest that we should all become holy and live like saints, but…

Believing they had a soul or that they are a spiritual being and the body is only a vessel, people in the past treated the body simply as the physical and actual representation of themselves, their souls, character, the essence of themselves. Therefore, they paid even more attention to it, albeit of a different kind to the attention paid today. The way people used to move, talk, dress, all had to be dignified and have some class. It is like when someone wants to represent himself better, he wears his best outfit. We all believe that clothes say something about a person.

Conversely, nowadays people believe there is nothing but the body – most don't believe in the existence of the soul – only that there might be some kind of awareness or mind, but that is still too much of an abstract concept for most people. We are in the age of cynicism; seeing is believing, and the body is no abstract, it is tangible. That makes it easy for people to believe that the body is all that exists and to dismiss any real possibility for the existence of the soul. Consequently, more attention is paid to the body and its emotions, feelings and needs.

The three main bodily needs are: sex, looks and nourishment.

Were we to someday fully embrace these notions, we would then be under the body's complete control and influence.

Most people still believe in values and look for a person of moral character to be with. Furthermore, the vast majority of women do not sleep around, and when they have had several partners it has normally been due to the attempt to find 'the one'. But if we continue in the direction we are heading in today, we may find both men and women becoming utterly soulless.

I do not believe, though, that all of the inhabitants of this planet will or could lose themselves to that degree. Instead I postulate that we will see a bigger division in cultures or with groups of peoples within cultures. The populace of this world consists of a majority who could be almost blindly led to a bitter end, but many have a strong moral compass and will remain virtuous, and it is these who will probably be forming communities and separate settlements within countries or states that will attempt to stay away from those who have almost completely given themselves to technology and the look-out-for-number-one and the take-care-of-the-body culture.

This is a very slippery slope, the more we submit to urges and quick thrills like sex, the more we actually validate them and the harder it is to stop. These feelings and thrills do not serve to enhance or enrich our human and spiritual sides, they cannot make us happy. Deep down inside we all know that – can you recall a time when you surrendered to the desire to have sex and regretted it the minute it was over? I sure can. That is why people who often submit to these short-term thrills and excitements can rapidly and increasingly become indifferent to these quick fixes. Eventually, it will even make them somewhat miserable and depressed. And at that point the more they continue on that road the more miserable they will become and the harder it will be for them to conjure the will and motivation to stop.

One of the main reasons for the spread of and the difficulty in stopping this growing trend with regards to sex and relationships is the problem of projection. We all project our thoughts, emotions and feelings from within. People sense what we are projecting. We are all aware beings and can easily spot someone who projects sexuality, for example, and one who does not. It is very easy to detect.

The more people give attention to sex; treating it as a means to satisfy an urge and as a central theme in their lives, the more it will be projected from them. As a result, more people will sense and perceive this and will therefore believe or naturally conclude that this has become more prevalent in society. That will either infect them and push them down the same road or will at the very least make them more despondent. The trouble is, young people growing up in this kind of society will most likely be pushed down that road rather than simply become despondent.

We do not want to become people who are viewed chiefly as pieces of meat to be used for sexual thrills. Many a woman knows the rather demeaning and terrible feeling of having been used for sex and nothing more.

The more spiritual you are (this doesn't necessarily mean religious) and the greater your belief in the existence of the soul, or simply substance, the more you understand your body as a vessel for yourself; to your character and virtue, and rather less a principal means for attaining quick and short-lasting thrills and emotions. The body is like a separate entity with its own needs and wants. An entity which is different from our souls; essence and substance, and often stands in contrast to it.

At present, we are at the stage where it has become the norm in most parts of the world to think more about one's needs as opposed to taking the long-term thinking approach and doing the just and right thing. This causes many a relationship and family to break apart fairly easily and quickly.

Living for the moment and not thinking in the long-term lead people to look for immediate thrills and fun. Many are excited about having different partners and fresh beginnings. I can understand the excitement to a degree. Beginnings, meeting a new person, can be thrilling. The trouble is, this fades quickly and then what? Can we keep living like that? Jumping from one thrill to another without constructing something more meaningful? (More and more men – and women too – think this is possible, but deep down inside we all know better).

Moreover, generally, the more we take sex and relationships lightly, the less special and exciting they are for us and the more blasé we become about them. I believe that it is much better, more productive and more gratifying to be excited about things, to appreciate things more. Appreciation is one of the most powerful and important emotions for the enjoyment of life and it acts as a catalyst for our drives towards the attainment of things in life.

The search for and the excitement from new beginnings, sex-based relationships or short-term relationships are in direct ratio to the legitimacy given to them by society; the degree of our agreement with it. In other words, the more society agrees with something, the more it will be acceptable and commonplace.

As a result of these changes, people today no longer believe they can maintain and sustain a true and life-long relationship. People used to get married and utter vows they believed in. Many today, even while standing at the altar, doubt the practicality and veracity of these promises.

It's getting to the stage where a very moral person is considered to be almost saint-like, and looked upon somewhat with disbelief and confusion.

As a consequence, at present, the lack of belief on women's part that men would fulfil their oaths and stand by their words is astonishingly wide-spread. It even feels to me at times, more often than not of late, that many women have trepidations about falling in love all together; worrying and expecting to get hurt after they do. This is not a new concept but it is much more widespread today. But if women will continue to contribute to this dwindling spiral of lack of trust and virtue by behaving like men, the plot will thicken and the overall situation for both sexes will become much grimmer.

As discussed earlier, the principal culprits for the continuous decline of our society in the subjects mentioned above are the music, film and TV industries, the media in general. What's more, these outlets' principal target-audience is mainly twelve- to sixteen-year-old girls and boys – when they are most vulnerable. Not only is the media content often deleterious but also many of the people whose faces and names we have come to know do not act or behave in their own private lives as good role models, to say the least.

A 'look-out-for-number-one' type of philosophy and the concentration more on looks and physicality make it much more difficult for all of us to find someone, fall in love with him/her and remain focused and loyal to that person. In view of this, the criteria for finding a person to have a relationship with have been changing in recent times. The idea and image of the potentially ideal partner for many at present were formed in the backdrop and settings of the society they grew up in, the society of the last twenty to thirty years. What kind of movies, music, TV series and role models were these last generations raised on? Well, you know the answer to that question. As a consequence, a lot of us today don't expect much from a relationship, at least in relation to longevity and complete fidelity. And that is also why, living in a world almost completely under the spell and control of the media, many of us strive for that easy, 'cool' and smooth type of relationship, like the ones depicted in many a series or movie, further pushing us away from maintaining a real relationship in real life – because real life is no movie.

More and more also dream of or desire to be with a good looking, cool, movie-star type of person. These are more infatuated with image than with actual, real-life people. The problem is that the vast majority of us don't look or act like a TV, movie, football or commercial star. As a result of all of the above, more people are suffering from poor self-esteem and low self-confidence, which makes it even more difficult to find and keep a relationship.

This current and evidently confusing reality makes it very hard to stay moral and preserve our values when more and more of those around us do not. Like when friends and the people we know enter into relationships lightly and have occasional and off-hand flings. A lot of men who do not want to think two steps ahead in life feel quite happy about this state of affairs and jump at the opportunity to date as many women as they possibly can, to have numerous sexual partners and encounters and by doing so lowering their own expectations of relationships even further (if men used to believe deep down that after all the dating, sex and adventures they would find someone to settle down with, now they are no longer even optimistic about that). This in turn infects the women they come in contact with and they, as a consequence expect less and less of men.

People maintain that it is normal for each new generation to feel different from the previous one, because attitudes, concepts and ideas are always changing and that it is normal for gaps to form. And it's also therefore not unusual for parents to not fully or truly understand their children. But since the inception of the internet and the surge in technology, whereby any idea or concept can be facilitated and spread quickly and easily, we have seen gaps forming, changes taking place and a general decline in social and human interactions which no generation or historic era has witnessed previously.

Affirmative action

The promoted and implemented reforms concerning equal rights and opportunities for women in recent times have been viewed by many women as an opportunity for some kind of light or silent social affirmative action. Some even relish the opportunity to not only try and be better, more successful and stronger than men, but to as well punish men and get back at them for their patronizing and demeaning behaviour and attitudes in the past and present. This is reasonable and predictable in a way, but it is also unproductive for both women and men. Affirmative action or punishment never work, whether sanctioned by government or solely in people's minds. Affirmative action only hurts those whose parents and grandparents were the offenders. It generates resentment and drives a wedge between the so-called villains and those who 'benefit' from the affirmative action. When you give someone a free meal while another eating in the same restaurant has to pay for it, both people would feel, to an extent, bad about it and also that this is unfair. The one who's having to pay for it would resent it, be upset and consider this unjust; "Why do I have to be discriminated against on account of my ancestors' behaviour?" He/she is also likely to feel resentment towards the person getting the meal for free – unless he/she chooses to view the beneficiary as a victim and supports that. In that case a whole set of other problems would kick in, namely, driving people into a 'victim' status and state of mind which will validate and give precedence to 'victimhood' type emotions over rationality, logic and healthy, motivational, positive and constructive type emotions – a state of affairs which has been growing rapidly around the world lately with devastating, deleterious effects. Pushing people into 'victim' status will also magnify division and inequality –- most people still believe, and would rather adhere to, concepts such as 'create your own destiny', 'take life in your own hands' and 'be a victor not a victim'.

A good analogy for this would be parents who adopted two boys choosing to pamper the older more than the younger because the former suffered in the care of his biological mother before he was adopted. How do you think that would make the younger child feel? By the same token, you don't punish a person whose grandfather was a thief. We don't levy more tax on or place last in line for college someone whose father was a rapist, right? The laws of the land, and the world for that matter, restrict reprehension and punishment strictly to the offender him/herself, to the one who committed the actual crime, which is basic logic! So why affirmative action??

Affirmative action is, to an extent, simply a reversal of the discrimination that went before. The 'green hats' were discriminated against by the 'blue hats', so now we will give more to the 'green hats' and basically discriminate against the 'blue hats'.

The person who gets something for free or generally has better conditions would also consider the act unjust and deep down inside (too deep inside at times) she/he will know that this is unfair. Like, for example, when someone pays cheaper tuition fees than his good friend and classmate. In what way will this make the person benefiting from this affirmative action a better person? Often this person doesn't even *think* any more about what happened in the past to his ancestors, let alone *feel* the injustices perpetrated upon them a generation or two before.

True, plenty of men still behave in ways that merit criticism and reprehension, but the upset and resentment of some women against men in the western world is mostly due to a long history of men being dominant and controlling – the accumulation of upset and anger through the ages, not necessarily because of a pure and objective analysis of men at present.

We can clearly see this happening in the US, for instance, where men are treated, judged and scrutinized more harshly in almost every aspect of their lives.

Giving free things to people, precedence over others, better conditions than their peers or simply better and more favourable treatment does not improve the characters or lives of these people in any shape or form. This normally would make one feel ungrateful, at times lazy or simply confused and/or at worst, drive him/her into victimhood. Affirmative action would definitely not assist in making our society more cohesive and just.

When a woman, or any person for that matter holds a grudge, that person is not truly free to love or feel, nor to have a productive and positive 'togetherness'.

We don't want to distance men and render them somewhat helpless, confused and then resentful. It won't be conducive to the futures of the two genders attempting to live together.

Buttons and our resolve

We all have buttons that can be pushed and elicit a response from us. When you see and smell a chocolate cake while you are on a diet, when your friends take you to a bar when you don't want to drink or when you see vivid images of people having sex in every second movie or half-naked people on many video clips and photos featured on various media outlets, these are pressing your buttons. These are directed at urges and wants which are not under our full control. Sex is a major button. We all possess basic biological needs and urges to reproduce, procreate, have sex. We also love being close to people and sharing the same space with someone we really like, love or feel attracted to. With enough repetition these strong urges and wants can be taken advantage of and manipulated in most people.

When, for example, concepts like one-night-stands and the easiness with which a person succumbs to one's urges when faced with temptation rather than be moral, virtuous, do the only right, just and fair thing and remain faithful to his/her spouse are being portrayed and shown more freely and openly on practically every type of media platform, our buttons regarding the subjects of sex, closeness, sense of adventure and the desire to do something wild or irresponsible are continuously being pressed. At the same time, these concepts are also mostly being portrayed as acceptable and 'cool', which then influences us on a long-term basis as well; it changes our minds with regards to these subjects.

The subjects of sex, attraction, physical passion and lust have apparently and evidently been pushed upon us from all directions and pretty much unceasingly in recent times. Many of us can still look back and remember how much better and simpler sex and relationship-related matters used to be fifteen, twenty or twenty-five years ago. The repercussions are everywhere and for anyone to see. Many of us would like to remain true to ourselves, keep a clear conscience and behave morally. But to remain so becomes much tougher and trickier when many around us do not. When we eventually succumb to pressure, as many of us unfortunately do, and let ourselves be influenced, behave or do something against our better judgment; compromise on our beliefs and integrity, we essentially open the door for further unprincipled behaviour or to compromise. We let our defences be breached to an extent and we become susceptible to more compromise. It then becomes harder to shut the door again, to go back to being principled and moral. I believe this happens because we now possess the knowledge that we capitulated and did something we did not like to do or agree with, this weakens our moral foundations and structure. Apparently keeping our integrity intact is so important to us that when we break it we feel like we fractured it for good.

For instance: when a girl who had been high-minded until her late twenties one night after a party and a few drinks succumbs to pressure: "come on, live a little, go have fun, don't be a nerd, he's cute", and sleeps with a guy she doesn't really know and who was not interested in anything but a one-night stand with her, she then fractures her integrity and opens the door to similar behaviour in the future; and the next time she's faced with the same situation her defences won't be as strong or effective, and a repetition of the same mistake could more easily occur. Indeed, some girls/women can stop there and go back to being moral and principled but I feel that this is not often the case.

Had one or two friends of this girl been principled and morally sound and have supported her high-minded approach there would have been a very good chance she wouldn't have gone and spent the night with this guy and possibly regret it the day after.

Ordinarily it is very hard to keep resisting some dogma, new concept or belief that has taken a hold of society. These social powers, pulling and pushing in a certain direction, making it tougher and tougher for one to continue to resist; it becomes hard work, tiring. Eventually most of us capitulate. Upon doing so we feel somewhat relieved, some pressure has been reduced, we don't have to walk against strong winds anymore. Once that's done it is doubly difficult to resume resistance; knowing that we have taken a turn which we do not really approve of, we don't like it. But just like when an enforced change occurs, when conditions and circumstances dictate a reality change for us, we accept and learn how to live with it. We find something to laugh about and make the best out of our lives in this new, not as good, current reality.

There is a big misconception in the minds of many, especially among young people – a lot of whom like to break the rules and be wild – that being irresponsible or impetuous and not thinking about the morrow is cool, being groovy or hip. Like when getting drunk, speeding or having a one-night stand. Many of them also consider being moral and right-minded to be too stern, not letting loose; being too serious, not living. That is far from being true. One can be wild, adventurous and very free in her/his demeanour and behaviour and still be principled and moral. The two don't, in the main, contradict one another.

As mentioned above, just one instance of lowering our standards and breaking our moral consciousness – even after fifteen, twenty or even thirty years of preserving our integrity – is usually enough to act as a small crack in a big dam holding back a huge amount of water. Eventually the crack will widen and then the dam breaks. In this day and age there is so much 'water' one fights to hold back in order to remain relatively principled and exemplary.

Therefore, when one's buttons are being pushed in order to arouse or provoke a reaction or a particular emotion, and one acts upon them against one's better judgment with regards to sex, alcohol or anything else, it won't be too long before these buttons won't have to be pushed so hard anymore in order to elicit a similar response. They will be basically, to one degree or another, pressed continuously. The reason for this is, when a person gives in and acts to the tune of a button, by doing so that person in actuality further pushes his or her button. This gives us the original push of the button; the manipulation by a different person, the media, movie, picture – or anything else for that matter – and then the subsequent magnification of the original push by the person her/himself; she/he accepted it, acknowledged it and acted upon it, and by having done so she/he actually has given it more power. Hence, by succumbing and acting on buttons which have been pressed, a person renders them doubly strong, widens the crack in his moral defences and makes her/himself more susceptible to future manipulation. This is even more complicated and entrapping when it happens to teenagers. A teenage girl, for example, not fully mature emotionally and mentally can fall into the trap of a trend – such as having sex freely and relatively indiscriminately – more easily than if she were six or seven years older. By so doing she risks impairing her self-image and confidence, which may affect her negatively in important aspects of life – I've seen it happen many times. The image one has of oneself is vastly important for one's social, married and personal life.

We as people then should think long and hard about how we want to raise our children, what values we want them to be brought up with and what tools, moral or behavioural, we need to instil in them in order for them to have the best possible start to their adult lives.

I don't want to sound too serious and gloomy. There are plenty of right-minded and principled people who remain so even when faced with hardship and social pressure. Moreover, no one will lose her/his life from acting irresponsibly once or twice. I would only like us to realize and be aware of the existing chance that, by acting irresponsibly and against our better judgment, we may be straying from the path we would like to stay on or initially set for ourselves. And when that happens and we do stray, it is only much later that we realize things haven't been going our way.

However, we can make things better. We can change and reverse any trend or situation we've got ourselves into. For this we should be strong, stand up for our values, applaud and openly appreciate someone who stands up for hers or his. We should also encourage more people to do so. When social pressure eases off a little – people lessening the pressure a bit and letting other opinions be expressed – time and space will free up for change to occur and more people will feel brave enough to keep their integrity intact and follow their beliefs. Our integrity, self-esteem, dignity and honour are extremely important for everything we do in life.

Carpe diem

In keeping with last century's mistaken belief that people are nothing more than a body made out of chemicals and no soul, a continually increasing number of people are thinking primarily about themselves and their fast-ending lives and looking to seize the day and provide themselves with as much fun, excitement and satisfaction as they can get. When one believes there is nothing after death, that one is nothing but a transient and fleeting being, one tries to get as much as one can from life in the time one has. Normally such person's long-term thinking ability would take a hit and her/his perspectives on just about anything under the sun would be reshaped accordingly. (Why think long-term when all will be finished soon anyway?) The trouble is, even if we do have the one life, we don't stay young, good-looking, vital and full of energy for the entire duration of that lifetime. Our youth and early adulthood pass fairly quickly. Seizing the day when it comes to sex and relationships will leave most of us alone and depressed in our older years. And I am pretty certain that each and every one of us upon inspection, honest inspection that is, would bemoan and regret the 'carpe diem' type of attitude we had had up until only a few years before. On the other hand, dedication, devotion, good deeds, morals and values, all resonate forever. Even if we die and it is all finished, our good and exemplary behaviour will definitely live on. It stays with the people who are still among the living, it shapes the way they view life and serves as a good model for posterity.

Sexy versus Graceful

Picture a chart of human attitudes and qualities going from best to worse. Which kind of attitude or quality would you rank highest?

Which would you rate higher on the chart, being graceful or sexy?

Honesty or infidelity?

Trust and faith (any type of faith, not necessarily religious) or cynicism?

Many women and men today try to be sexy. The way they dress, move about, talk or do things. There is, too, the not-so-obvious way of being sexy – the projection of sex; the transmission of sexual thoughts and desires by one's own thoughts and comportment – we, as people, sensitive and intuitive creatures, can sense intentions; even with only the subtlest physical manifestations, women pick up men's intentions very quickly. Women who try to be sexy do so for various reasons; as a means to an end, simply because it is acceptable, purely in order to tease men and/or to receive affirmation as a woman. Men do so mostly for, well, it's pretty obvious. This attitude is roughly the opposite of being graceful and classy and would rank lower on our chart of human attitudes and qualities. (This book is about femininity; therefore, we will be focusing more on women in this chapter).

A woman is sexiest when she is not trying to be sexy! The reason why projection of sex would be low on the chart is because projection of sex is done with the obvious intent of pressing buttons; attempting to affect or influence someone or something in a manipulative manner. Pressing our sex-related buttons will not be viewed as or considered a classy behaviour in the eyes of the vast majority of objective people. We are all easily able to sense when someone is trying to influence or manipulate us in such a way as to elicit a response from us. Most of us genuinely don't like or appreciate this.

A woman is sexiest when she is simply being feminine and asexual in public. This is a deadly combination (being asexual is actually part of what femininity is, but we will break it down just for the sake of simplicity and emphasis.) What we have here then is a beautiful feminine creature and at the same time no projection of sex.

As a side remark, I believe that any woman who's feminine and graceful, who's taking basic care of herself physically is to some extent beautiful, regardless of her facial features, her hair type or style.

We all know that sex is a big push-button for men, as well as for woman – albeit only to a degree. Using sexual behaviour in order to manipulate and get something out of someone is almost always cheap. When we attempt to manipulate or push buttons we are basically declaring that we don't regard or take the person opposite us or the people around us seriously enough, that we're not trying to appeal to the real person, his/her psyche, character, mind, intelligence and his/her better judgment or objective self, but to that person's lower-level emotions and urges; buttons. Many women unfortunately believe that this is a natural and good way to get the attention of men.

I do not mean, in this chapter, to harshly criticize women or men who act or behave sexily. I have no problem, anger or resentment towards them. Nor do I wish for us to be strict and over-scrutinize the subject. No, all and everything should be a personal choice! Freedom of expression should always be the most precious and adhered-to concept. However, I wish to convey a point a view which I believe many share and by that perhaps raise our personal awareness with regards to this subject to the point where we try to better our society and make it one which is based on reason and substance rather than looks and physical attraction.

As far as I can ascertain, every man would prefer his woman (and vice versa) not to project sex in public. Sure, men like it when they are on the prowl, looking for a one-night stand or for a sex-based relationship. But no man, or woman, would want his/her partner to be projecting sex in public. When a woman does not project sex in public it primarily means that she considers sex to be an intimate thing, not a cheap thing to show off with or play with. That woman views sex as a more personal and private thing to be shared between two people. This would generally mean that when that woman becomes intimate with a man, that man has the whole of that woman, she is fully with him and it is very personal and meaningful. I believe all us would prefer that.

Intimacy is the difference between sex done by two specific people with some affinity towards each other and a personal touch, and sex done in a mechanical way between two people who have nothing more than a sexual desire to exchange.

Sex with intimacy is done between two individuals. Sex without intimacy and purely for the act itself is done by two bodies run by individuals.

Lots of women think that being sexy – which according to the current social definition is projecting sex (the use of body movements, facial expression and gaze as sexual innuendos and insinuations, attempting to push buttons) and showing skin – is part of being feminine. Well, that's true only when society gives sex more attention than it does virtue. Seventy years ago, the vast majority of people would have considered that cheap. Today, the number of people who would is most probably much lower. Meanings and definitions of terms change with time. Femininity in the purest and most classical manner is all the things we've talked about earlier in this book – a woman is sexy enough without attempting to be sexy.

What does being sexy even mean? Sexy solely means attractive, being sexy means being physically attractive. Therefore, when a man is looking to have sex or for a sex-based relationship he will find a woman sexy when she behaves in accordance with the currently prevailing definition of sexy. When one is looking for love and regards character, persona and substance as the most important attributes of a person, that person will find a woman to be sexy and most appealing when she refrains from behaving in the ways that are considered sexy these days. Thus, women who are attempting to be sexy, in the newer sense of the word, will be regarded fairly cheaply in his eyes.

For me personally, a woman who's showing interest in a man by giving him an innocent "I'm interested in you" look or smile, is the most appealing, the most attractive and sexiest.

These days, both genders project more and more sex and are increasingly concerned with physical attraction. Many men toss mental and physical sexual innuendos at women, often at women who are already involved and with no regard to their marital status. I'm certain that the men who do so would hate it if anyone else did that to the ones they love. We must return to a respectful and considerate behaviour and keep sexual innuendos and insinuations strictly to people and times when we're sure they're relatively appropriate.

I suppose we can all agree that it would be horrible to live in a society where women and men can no longer have an innocent conversation, one without sexual innuendo, attempts to be sexy or appear attractive or attempts to elicit responses and reactions from one another. We are still far from that point and many people acknowledge that, refrain from this kind of behaviour and exhibit respect and dignity. Nevertheless, we should be vigilant and make certain it doesn't go there.

You are what
you believe you are

Being yourself, truly yourself is a very attracting quality. Add grace and class to it – as long as it's done naturally – and you have a beautiful thing, a winning formula.

A person is treated by others in the same fashion that she/he treats and thinks of her/himself! When you respect yourself and believe that you are a good person, that is how people will view you and treat you. When you think of yourself as being weak, insecure or unsuccessful as a person, guess what, that is how you will be regarded and treated. People pick up on what we project and primarily act according to that.

Women! You are the better sex! Be yourselves, don't sell yourself short or diminish yourselves by trying to be and act like men.

Alas, many these days do. "It's a phase we have to go through until things settle", some will say. True, times of change, like we've had with women's rights in recent decades, are often accompanied by some confusion and disorder. Yet it doesn't have to be chaotic or deleterious to us as a society. Disorder and confusion can be kept to a minimum if we just keep our resolve and cool. In addition, many women use these changes and try to be or to demonstrate that they are better and stronger than men and that they don't really need men anymore.

Emasculation of men is a major issue at present in some parts of the world and it has major repercussions. By taking the place of men in some matters where men expect themselves to be the prime doer – where they have been for thousands of years – we're causing men to become bewildered and psychologically unbalanced. This is a lose-lose situation. The results of which can already be felt: men are confused, not sure of how to be, act, behave and as a consequence are less assertive, less emotionally stable for themselves and for the woman they're with and are increasingly insecure. I can hear the cries of many a woman lamenting that ever-expanding actuality. I can also see *men's* empowerment programmes in the very near future, trying to repair the damage.

One detrimental effect of this recent phenomenon can already be seen in the confusion many men share when it comes to the pursuit of women; the making advances to and the way to behave and act at the early stages of the relationship. Women today are very hard to predict, they act in many unpredictable ways which make many men today afraid to even approach them. Many women are stuck between being feminine, strong-minded, hard-to-get, independent and polite. These can produce a myriad of reactions from them when approached by men. Being independent and the projection of that makes many men feel unneeded or unwanted to a degree. Post-modern and independent attitudes can also mean that the man is not expected to be the sole pursuer or initiator, and that makes the whole subject of pursuit yet again complex. Men today are required to be strong, understanding, modern and gentlemen at the same time. Many don't pass the test and drop out of the race. Obviously, this in turn has a deleterious effect on women. As we've recently been able to see, more and more are agitatedly waiting for the 'right' man to show up. In the past when the roles were much clearer, things were much simpler, better and more conducive to the lives of both genders. Also, no matter how 'advanced' we think we are at present, most women would still like their men to at least be able to be strong and protective when needed, in the old-fashioned way. Wars, violent conflicts and hardship are no distant memory. Most, whether showing that or not, would expect and want their men to be men when the situation arose.

Therefore, maintaining a balance is imperative! An acknowledgment that both genders equally need one another is vitally important and a better understanding of the role each plays can be very beneficial.

Here is an example of the kind of thinking prevalent with some women today: I've met some who get really irritated when I, or any man for that matter, open the door for them. To these women, in their minds, the act of a man being a gentleman, opening the door for a woman means *the past* and equals the old times when women were oppressed and suppressed, when women were considered inferior. They're so passionately looking to put the past behind them, resisting so hard, that they cannot distinguish a simple act of kindness from the horrible past.

That being said, everyone should do whatever she/he wants to do and whatever feels right to her/him! But I believe no woman needs to get upset, resentful or perhaps defensive when things like "men are physically stronger", "they can do a particular sport better", "they are different to women in that respect", "they can fix things", "they drive better" and so on, are being mentioned? There are so many things you, women, do better than men! We men accept that. We have no problem with that. Most of us know that you are the better sex, even though many would not admit to it. That is what makes life interesting and challenging: differences. And yes, you can be great drivers and at times even better than men!

Once, a long time ago, I got injured and had to be rushed to the hospital. My girlfriend at the time stepped right up to the mark and took the wheel. In the midst of moving about in the passenger seat trying to get more comfortable and to control my pain and anguish, I couldn't help but notice and admire the way the car was moving quickly and under great control and ease through the twists and turns in the road. Upon quick reflection I concluded that the girl beside me was a better driver than me. And I'm a very skilful driver.

Driving, like many other things in life, is an acquired skill. It takes practice and requires the indoctrination of the person in question to the attitudes and approaches which relate to the subject at hand or any given subject. Most girls, while growing up, emphasize different things than boys; they tend to the more delicate and gentle matters in life and mostly with a feminine attitude. Boys are traditionally expected to be able to fix, operate and run things, use their muscles and also to be able to take care of themselves and handle the various random and difficult situations that may arise. Furthermore, most of the jobs which require physical strength are still held by men, generally providing men with more orientation with regard to the physical world. Many men around the world also join the army or military, and some even prepare for that type of life years in advance. This again gives them more command in physically-related matters. Historically, men's sense of direction and orientation have been developing for eons. Men were always outdoors doing whatever being outdoors entailed. Work, trade, travel, fighting battles. Even the driving of vehicles was a thing done predominately by men up until 50 years ago. In addition, men usually put a lot of emphasis on how they drive; it is almost a tacit requirement but nonetheless a requirement that men be good at driving. We would not admit it or talk about it normally, but handling a car and oneself on the road say something about a man, and when done well pamper most men's egos. Many of us also like to show off and be mischievous on the road. Men compete in almost anything they do. Woman, as in most things, are more practical and mature in attitude and approach and most often use a car to take them from point A to point B. This is not a bad thing; it is essentially safer and more productive. Furthermore, as I said, women do many things better than men. You don't usually hear men lamenting that fact.

Women are more

Let's return our attention to what is essentially the main argument of this book: women, why reduce yourselves to the level of men and try to match men in sex, relationships and courtship, in attitude and approach, forsaking grace and class, trying to prove that you can do everything men can and turning your backs on gentlemanliness? I'm sure most of you would probably never attempt these things if you weren't consciously and subconsciously wrongly trying to compete with men or to express your resentment for yesteryear. You were never inferior to men! You were merely considered to be inferior. You don't need to prove anything to anyone, just be yourselves. The natural you. You need not do things the way men do. The way you naturally do things is more graceful and more beautiful, and it is also essential and crucial to the world we live in. What's more, this idea that you must be equal and everything should be equal can keep you in a state of constant alert and make you touchy and over-sensitive to many a thing. Should a man say or do something that may suggest chauvinism or old-fashioned behaviour, you might go into attack mode or become defensive. That is not a productive way to live nor have a relationship. The striving and quest for equal rights and opportunity is of the highest importance! But equal to men? Why, when you are naturally more?

You have the advantage of being feminine and with that you have the great power of being womanly. Femininity has an incredible power over men, almost like a spell. It has power over other women too. Many women platonically appreciate a graceful and classy woman and consider her to be a beautiful thing. A feminine woman can achieve so much with a little smile, by stroking her hair or just by being graceful or elegant. Why take your amazing, unique features and characteristics and blunt them? Strength, muscles, toughness and casual sex are inferior to beauty, class – femininity!

Gentleness and delicateness are superior to physical force or toughness.

Grace and class are much higher virtues than being 'cool' and physical self- satisfaction.

A soft caress can achieve, and usually does, much more than a slap on the wrist or across the face. People respond to 'gentle' and 'nice' more than they do to force or toughness. Ah, you may say, some would respond uniquely to force; well, that is true, but even these people would resent, be it openly or strictly internally, the force directed at them. Deep inside they would appreciate a gentle approach much more – yet, at times force is necessary only because they themselves cannot control their own urges.

Being gentle is stronger than being strong!

Casualness and its consequences

Virtue and values are innate to people. As surprising as that may sound, they are.

People are basically good and they want to do unto others what they would like to have done unto them. But we all also possess the urges, needs and desires of our selfish self and the body, which can come into conflict with virtue.

A child or a teenager growing up immersed in a society that advocates largely unvirtuous or immoral behaviour, or one which simply turns a blind eye and accepts that kind of behaviour – like in our present society in general – will find it very difficult to maintain or exhibit good values and act upon them.

The reason many women have been going down the road of questionable behaviour (questionable not only by an outside observer but by themselves also) is partly because they simply can and largely because they want to shake off the shackles placed on their ankles by men until not so long ago. After you have been imprisoned for a while, or a long while, upon your release you want to run in an open field and embrace every aspect of freedom available, especially when it is encouraged and supported by an increasing number of people who have begun to think similarly. It is understandable. But when you're messing with sex and relationships you're messing with dynamite and gunpowder.

Women were the more sensible and prudent gender from since we can remember; throwing all that to the wind and replacing common sense and long-term thinking with the ever-expanding current state of affairs is immensely unfortunate.

Embracing freedoms and liberties and going against the ways of the past can be so all-encompassing that plenty of virtues and values are liable to be neglected or forgotten altogether. I do not necessarily believe that a woman should remain a virgin until her wedding night. But I do believe that plentiful sex partners and relationships do not contribute in any shape or form to women. And the same for men!

It is disheartening to see how young girls and boys behave today in schools and colleges. Up until fifty years ago, chastity was a word that meant something, it was considered a virtue. Today this word is hardly used anymore. It's a shame to see the way youth has come to view virginity. It is almost a thing of ridicule in some parts of western cultures. Losing your virginity used to mean something and was of greater importance some twenty, thirty or forty years ago.

Whole cultures today, mainly western, are near to reaching the point where promiscuity as a term barely applies anymore. In these cultures, cheating is regarded pretty much as a regular and normal thing. It's still considered bad and unvirtuous but increasingly much less frowned-upon and criticized than it used to be some fifty years ago, or even ten.

Such a state of affairs is providing people with a wider and more comfortable platform on which they can display and act upon their urges and sexual desires, with no regard for people's feelings or for the sake of their own relationships, and without truly being reprehended for it, either.

Circumstances have undoubtedly changed of late, and as a consequence, the vast majority of us have more than one sex partner before we get married. Normally these days we go through a few or several relationships before we settle, hopefully, on the one. In addition, sex is being emphasized more, and as a result plays a bigger role in many people's lives these days.

As it relates to sex – the quality and enjoyment of – as a general rule I can pretty much guarantee that when one is after sex only, as in one-night stands or sex-based relationships, the more partners that person has the less and less she/he will be able to enjoy sex! Conversely, the more respectful, sensible and tactful one is with his body and matters related to sex, the more that person will be appreciated and appreciate her/himself. In turn, sex will be more enjoyable for her/him and the one she/he is with. We enjoy being with someone we appreciate and respect more than with someone whom we don't so much.

Most people know that they are more than just flesh, and when they engage in sex just for sake of sex it feels cheap, and they usually are aware of this. The more one does so, the cheaper, less exciting and less special one will feel with regard to sex and with regard to him/herself. Therefore, the desire for more of it and the enjoyment derived from it will reduce as well. Whether it be after three, five or ten encounters for women or ten, twenty or a hundred for men.

By the way, one could still be anxious about having it, as are many, but anxiety is something entirely different than enjoyment or real passion.

The importance of sex between two in a relationship has risen in direct ratio to the rise in the emphasis put on the subject. I believe we should not put too much emphasis on sex when we are in a relationship or when looking for one. We all obviously want to have a great sex life. Yet, if we haven't, it's definitely not the end of the world. Other matters are more important for the sustainment of a good relationship. But we can have a great sex life as well. We can learn how to better our sex lives even with someone who doesn't initially seem to be good or compatible. Learning about one another, and from the experience together, can make a huge difference.

Many women have never had great or even very good sex in their lives. It is quite common and remarkable at the same time to learn from them that they rarely reached orgasm and that their past partners didn't really understand them in bed, nor were they good lovers. This is due to the lack of willingness, mainly on the part of men, to learn and improve coupled with the misconception that the knowhow with regards to performance in bed should come to us pretty much naturally. This is far from being true! Like anything else in life, the more we learn about and have experience in a particular field the better we will be and do at it. By listening to one another and wanting to learn and improve, any couple can have a very good or even great sex life.

A compatible partner in character, perspectives and goals for life is much more important in the grand scheme of things. Placing our emphasis and attention on love, caring and on the strength of our bond – and of course the family – will form a beautiful relationship and will in turn make our sex life also better, more enjoyable and last for much longer than if we were in a relationship that is not based mostly on love, caring and family, even if it did have a great sex life. (A great sex life doesn't last long when the more important things mentioned above receive less or only equal attention as sex.)

In spite of

In spite of all the decline in values in recent times, women still exhibit much more self-restraint when it comes to sexual partners than do men. Women haven't completely lost their moral compass and more often than not when a woman changes partners she is actually looking for the one, hoping that this time the guy will be serious and view her as more than just a sex partner, object or a temporary companionship. (Even when she tells you that she is in it for the thrills and she's not looking for anything serious at the moment. Rare is the woman who truly feels that way.) Still, an increasing number of women have joined the trend of decline. some because they want to keep up, stay with the programme and not go against the grain. Others, after a short time in the marketplace, realizing what many men are like these days – and presumably many women too – come to not expect much and suppress their own true wishes to a greater or lesser extent. They then try to act and behave according to this 'cool' and prevalent attitude which says that sex doesn't have to mean much, it can be only sex and just for the fun of it and thus going along with the wishes of many men having flings or sex-based relationships. In reality, most women look for something meaningful and serious. Unfortunately, an increasing number of women are losing contact with their true selves and are therefore no longer aware of what they are looking for or really want.

Sometimes, though, a woman will sleep with a guy merely for affirmation as a desired woman.

Still in general, a big change in attitudes has occurred and women today are much quicker to go to bed with men. This has given rise to another phenomenon, or perhaps I should say has made it much more prevalent. A woman dating a man hoping he is serious would sleep with him after their second, third or fifth date and then the guy would leave, having got what he was trying to get, leaving her with no other option but to move on and try with another guy.

Jumping into bed early and quickly does not promote good, healthy and trustworthy relationships; it only gives men more chances to 'score' and more opportunities to further feed the ever-growing sentiment of distrust women share with regards to men. Most women know this but often these days succumb to pressure and what is considered 'normative' behaviour.

Attachment

Imagine how unfortunate it would be if women were similar to men on an emotional level. Women are generally more emotional, they cry more often and, most importantly, they get attached and fall in love faster and more frequently; most women only require a couple of good dates, great conversation or one night of lovemaking to feel attached and to start developing emotions towards a man. Their hearts and minds are quickly drawn to loving and to the feeling of attachment. They are built like that, thank goodness! I dread a world so shallow where everyone is unstable, shaky and unreliable with regards to feelings and emotions like many, many men are.

Women, being basically monogamous and serious with regard to relationships, often go to great lengths to try and make men like them. Many a woman uses subtle forms of provocation in order to get the attention of men. Others also utilize not-so-subtle ways. They dress sexily or show a little more than they would like to or use any one of the methods they are familiar with to get the attention of the man they like and in order to get him to make advances to them. Apart from the times when a woman does so simply to reaffirm her powers and influence as a woman – women are expected to be fetching and desirable – this is done in the hope that she and the guy will end up going on a date and spending some quality time together, so that she can maybe evoke real emotions from him towards her, get him to like something about her as an individual with character and substance, something more than the initial attraction that was provoked. Some even have sex with men if only to try and get them to have deeper feelings towards them.

That is not a criticism, it is more an observation. I do believe, though, that in most cases these methods are not really necessary nor they will be successful. Women should aim for a guy who is interested in the real person that she is, one who does not need to be lured in by physical attraction-evoking behaviour, sexual insinuations or innuendo. Women will have better chances of real success that way.

A word about monogamy

A woman's attitudes towards life are the more proper ones. A woman's feelings, stances and approaches towards relationships, children, violence, sex and just about everything under the sun are generally superior to these of a man.

Women cheat less than men (it used to be *a lot* less, up until recently) and very often for different reasons. When I say that to people, many of them reply: "Oh, you don't know", "That's not true", "I know a few who have", and so on, yet when I ask for specifics they can usually recall one, some may recall two or three examples; more often than not, though, on further investigation it turns out that in the vast majority of cases the man cheated on the woman first or simply treated her badly before she decided to cheat on him. People mostly don't even listen to the words I use – "less" – they instantly switch into cynic mode, which is basically a defensive one and, in actuality, blab out their own frustrations about the subject and about people and life in general by saying what they just have. It's also fashionable to be a cynic in this 'modern' world. This mainly stems from people's basic fear of getting hurt. Most of us subconsciously believe that to be cynical, and therefore have no real expectations of people, makes us more resilient and less fragile or sensitive in the face of disappointment or any other hurtful act towards us than if we were innocent or naive, in which case it would come more as a shock and would be more impactful. On top on that basic fear lies another fear, the fear of being told one specific sentence: "Don't be so naive!". For many that's a grave insult. They feel like they are being ridiculed. They don't want to be equated with someone who has no experience in life, someone who is like a child in mind, one who cannot see what people 'really' are; a naive person. These days if you are not 'naïve' and you know that people can't be trusted – and thus not to expect much of them – you're then considered normal, grown-up, even 'cool'.

Despite the fact that women are generally much better at being loyal, the more that betrayal and the act of cheating are legitimized, coupled with the ever-growing emphasis on sexual needs, wants and their satisfaction, the more women will cheat for no 'justified' or at least understandable reasons

I believe all people are monogamists in their core. While men are mostly disconnected from their real core substance, as human beings women are much more in touch with it. Therefore, women are almost automatically and naturally inclined to monogamy, to a lifelong relationship based upon dedication, devotion, fidelity and the building and developing of something substantial. Women are more concerned with raising a family, providing for their offspring and keeping things stable than the average man is. As a general rule, women are much more stable than men with respect to almost anything in life.

Still, if many men are monogamous in actuality, the rest can be too. This, for instance, can be shown by the fact that when it comes to their football team, the one they support, they adamantly and fanatically follow that same team their whole lives. They believe that once their love and support for the team are given they should obviously be lifelong. It is very clear and basic to them that they should remain loyal to that team come rain or come shine. Humans admire loyalty and try to be loyal where and when they can. Moreover, consider the fact that when in love we do not (men and women alike under any circumstances) like our loved one to be touched in any way that may convey intimacy by anyone else. Why would we care if we weren't possessive that way? Especially hard is when our partner cheats on us with another or even when he/she dates another straight after or shortly after we've separated; it can be really upsetting. And also, why would any break-up be hard and painful if we weren't monogamists??? Think about it! Especially when someone falls out of love with us – once love (dedication, devotion) is given we essentially and naturally expect it to remain. We are built like that. That is one reason why memories of break-ups stay with us and have power over us. Indeed, not all break-ups are hard. A break-up is tough in direct ratio to the level of love that existed between the two and to the strength of the connection and the bond between them. One can argue then that people are principally monogamous as long as they love one another. I don't believe it is necessarily dependent on that. If as long as one is in-love one is being monogamous and then when one is no longer in-love he/she is less inclined to remain monogamous, it means that the problem lies not necessarily in monogamy but in the reasons why one would love less or no-more after a period of time and how that will affect him/her. After all, the inclination to become less of a monogamist mostly appears *after* one falls out of love and not the other way around.

When we are in love, we are obviously happier, more excited about life, we look at things more positively and we are more purposeful. Most of our actions then are more of a positive nature, even if only a little, than when we are not in-love. When we feel this strong and positive emotion, especially when it is reciprocated, the *true* nature of us regarding actions we take and things we do and the ways in which we behave is shown. Our true nature is *not* shown when we are unhappy, sad or upset. Everyone is nice and positive when she/he is happy you say… Exactly my point! People are good and positive in their core, and that is why when all is good and well only then are we free to exhibit our *true* nature and intentions and behave in ways we *really want* and *choose* to – and in the vast majority of times we choose to be positive and good.

Monogamy is a very positive thing to uphold, it gives and shows another or a whole family dedication and devotion. It is much more likely that one would remain monogamous when one's disposition is good, contented or happy. Thus, the reasons why people are not monogamous don't lie in their lack of ability to remain monogamous, but elsewhere. I believe if couples had the tools, the knowhow and the motivation to make their relationships successful, happy and productive, the love and contented dispositions of both involved would be sustained and maintained for much, much longer and the bond between the two would be strong to a degree where monogamy could be easily and gladly achieved.

Considering all of the above, I'm therefore able to draw one conclusion only: people are basically monogamous and generally believe in fidelity. Hence, humans are *capable* of being monogamous and optimally should be.

Some are still old-fashioned

A word about my life at present and the society in which I live. I reside in Cracow, Poland. One of the reasons I chose to live here was how feminine the women are here, the most I've seen so far.

Polish society seems to have settled into a very good condition and fine balance after long, arduous and trying times for a century or two. Feminism as a movement was as big here as in other countries in the world but these days most women don't seem to worry about that anymore, and they don't truly need to either. Strong past movements of feminism combined with other major factors like religion, a history of tolerance and the belief in gentlemanliness, have brought this society to a relatively great place at present!

It is also still a relatively and positively old-fashioned society in many respects. In my opinion the balance between women and men here is simply stunning! It is in the perfect form and state. Women are allowed to be feminine, while men mostly treat women in the old-fashioned and beautiful way known as gentlemanliness. I've never seen such amazing female power and ascendency while being at the same time fully feminine, fully herself. I've seen countries where women are strong but they are no longer very feminine, they act strong and tough and demand their place in the world believing that this is the best way to go about achieving it.

Women in Poland are treated with a little more care and respect than men, as they should. The respect is given not because of fear of repercussion or because everyone *must* treat women so, nor because women constantly demand respect. The respect for women here is much more fundamental and ingrained in society, it comes naturally to most men. There seems to exist a tacit understanding and consent that women are to be respected and be held in the highest esteem. They, women, are treated with real appreciation and are regarded as a thing of beauty and desire.

These statements are not by all means true for every woman and man here. I've seen exceptions and I'm sure that there are many more. But as a general rule that is the case in this country. This also does not mean that women here are not concerned with other aspects of men, men's behaviour and relationships. Many of the ailments relationships are infected with, though less prevalent, are nevertheless in existence here.

Unfortunately, even here things have taken a turn for the worse and in a matter of only a few years women have become less feminine and are losing their feminine inclinations. These days physical borders can no longer keep away the tentacles of influence coming from over yonder, for better or worse.

'Progress' and new paradigms

'Progress' or 'modern' are two terms which are usually regarded as 'cool'. Progressive or modern attitudes are more often than not completely embraced by people as 'the-next-new-thing', the new way of thinking, the right way of thinking. People get a kick out of ridiculing the past or the old, making remarks like: "Man, that's old", "You're living in the past", "Get with the programme", "Get with the times". To 'live' in the past or remain old-fashioned is not 'cool' for one reason or another. It is interesting how people will always choose or lean towards supporting a new thing almost blindfold, with no real inspection of the facts. For most, 'new' means progress and they equate that word with better. Just like when a 'new' product comes out and people automatically assume it is better and they are more inclined to purchase that one over the old version of it. This phenomenon is more apparent with youngsters but it's very much the case with older people as well.

There is something odd about this, yet it is understandable to a degree – we like the concept of advancing. Standing still normally feels awkward and against the 'run of play' to us. Going backwards definitely feels so, to most of us. The future and the new always seem more promising and exciting. Some people love to reminisce, glorify the past and speak of it romantically; still, given the choice to go back and live in the past again they will choose to stay in the present and keep moving forward.

This sentiment causes many to almost immediately turn a blind eye towards something that up until very recently was accepted and commonplace, but is now no longer accepted or is frowned upon. Often, we do so against our better judgment, but with time we convince ourselves otherwise; we adapt to that new accepted reality. By doing so we often lose a part or all of this 'old' thing and the few or many benefits it contained.

Monogamy, for instance, is but one example; or should I say anti-monogamy? More and more people, though still not a huge number, even show off and take pride in not being monogamous. They feel that the new trend is better because it is newer and modern. Even people who still believe in monogamy dare not speak loudly and openly about it anymore. This is due to another force that's at play here; the fear or lack of courage, or the inclination on the part of the individual to go against this 'advancing' force and against what is accepted or considered 'in' at any particular point in time. This is a very sweeping and destructive force; the fear of contesting the new trend or going against the grain, the 'being-part-of', being like everyone else and joining the eagerness of the ones already submerged in it. This force has a snowball effect more often than not and it silences people, causes them to be fearful of the mob, fearful of being reprehended, ridiculed or scolded in public.

Political correctness is another great example of these forces at work. the term's original definition, which referred to POLITICAL correctness only, has changed and currently encompasses all kinds of 'correctness'. Most people upon serious introspection would realize what a destructive force political correctness can be. As little as five years ago, people could say things or tell jokes that today many would resent, rise up against or feel self-conscious or embarrassed about: "You can't say that", "That's racist", and so on. Here again, the majority of us, to one extent or another, has forsaken what existed and was prevalent only a few years before, our freedom of speech and expression and the right to have and practice our sense of humour. We then accepted a reality that most of us deep down resent. Still, we largely can't even feel that resentment anymore, nor can we think logically about the subject either. We are too submerged in this forward-moving force and in our inability to go against the grain, against what's considered current, 'in', 'cool'; the new and modern thing.

Yet another example would be the growing trend in drugs use, namely Marijuana. Twenty or thirty years ago everyone knew that Marijuana is a drug like any other drug: dangerous and bad for one's health. Today, most believe it is ok, not addictive and even has some health benefits. Sure, there've been many papers and people advocating for it, but most people haven't investigated, learnt or read about the subject; they've simply followed the new trend and now they believe in it wholeheartedly.

Marriage and family

Concepts, ideas, beliefs and realities across the board have been changing, at times too sharply, for women and men both this past century. Two central aspects of life which have seen major changes in recent times are the age at which women and men get married and the level of eagerness to have children and a family.

Feeling free to do what they want to; with less in the way of social restraints and stigmas, along with the progressive and irresponsible music, movie and TV industries; the media in general, more and more women are considering marriage, children and family institutions as less and less relevant, as something to perhaps have later, "After I live a little", "After I finish university, get a job", "Make a career for myself" or a simple "I'm not interested in marriage and children". This comes as a direct result of the movement towards the individuation, introversion and care-of-the-body paradigms talked about before in this book, which manifest themselves in various ways but mainly in the forms of less compromise, less long-term thinking and a declining belief in the family unit.

One of the illusions or misconceptions this contemporary reality has given rise to is that a family is quite difficult to attain and retain if one wants to 'live' or have a successful career, pushing back the age at which people marry. As a result, some never get to marry because they 'missed the train' while others are no longer interested in marrying altogether. At present we are seeing more and more single older women, some too old to have children and start a family. I meet a lot of them, pushing forty with not much to be feeling great about. Some are still in the search for a partner, some have already given up on the idea completely. But even the ones that are still looking – dating sites on the net are filled with women and men searching – I don't believe they know what they are looking for exactly, except that they don't want to be alone anymore.

Not all or even most single women have chosen to still be single at forty; many of them haven't been able to find 'the one' due to the many ailments current society is suffering from and already mentioned throughout this book. But indeed, an increasing number of women and especially men of late are showing less and less interest in marrying and having children.

But at forty, an age at which most of us have usually already reached our comfort zones in terms of work and finances, and have already got used to living more on our own than with a partner; having catered to our own needs and only ours for such a long time, we become much choosier and less able to compromise. In addition, we have by now accumulated so many failed attempts at relationships and have 'learnt' so much about how people, especially men, cannot really be trusted and all they want and care about is sex and do not really care for a true and candid long-term relationship. All of the above makes it really hard to find someone with whom we can truly believe that it is possible to build, plan and go the distance.

It's true that in the past things were also far from perfect. Women got married early, often against their will, started a family and their paths in life were pretty much set. Women today are fully aware of that history; many have observed it at first hand, and are therefore mostly trying to stay away from it. Yet, they overlook the pluses and advantages that exist in the old ways. For starters, when you marry young your children will be grown when you are still relatively young, making the whole process of upbringing easier, more fun and enjoyable for both children and parents alike. This is mainly due to the fact that relatively young parents are able to relate to and understand their children more and be more of a friend to them than they would if they were older and the difference in ages were bigger. Second, once you're married, you've finished with the search for a partner, a search that can consume a lot of your time and effort. A search that could take quite long and be filled with heartbreak and the kinds of disappointment that commonly render us more cynical and less happy and optimistic. When we are young we are still relatively untouched, not yet cynical and with our hearts intact. It is much easier to build and have a relationship with these credentials as opposed to the mental and emotional resumé we carry everywhere with us when we are older. Young, we can choose and make decisions more wisely, yes young not older and with 'experience'. I know it sounds strange and goes against the prevailing dogma and current belief. When, for instance, a woman has had five failed attempts at relationships and she's approaching the age when she can no longer get pregnant, her decision-making processes will hardly be objective. They will be based more on cynicism, disbelief and time constraints. This is one of the reasons why we see a growing number of women bringing children into the world out of wedlock: they feel too old to find someone; basically, they don't really believe they could anymore and time is running out.

Some obviously meet and start healthy and successful relationships when they are older. But the older you get, the less are the chances of realizing your ideal relationship.

I believe that many of the divorces among couples who got married in their early twenties are not because they did so too young, but due to continuous pressure from society: the constant 'examples' of being single, living a life of relative no-accountability and the 'freedoms' that come from not having a partner and/or a family. That pressure acts more heavily on young people than people in their late twenties and thirties. One of the positive attributes most of us possess between the ages of twenty-five and forty is being more assertive and able to sustain relatively more pressure from our surroundings.

If society were to *support* marriage at any age many more couples who married relatively young would remain married.

Family and career

There is this inherent, unconditional connection, love and care in a mother-child relationship that nothing in life as we know it can surpass. Not even the most romantic and loving relationship is as pure as the relationship between a mother and child.

In my opinion, we are today living through more fragile and perilous times than in most periods of history for the past two or three millennia. No matter how wild and crazy matters used to be at certain points in the past, people have always had the family unit as a personal pillar of strength and as the very basic building block of their cultures. The fabric of society was held in place and supported by the family unit.

I can pretty much guarantee you that no woman (or man), no matter how successful a career she has, will feel truly accomplished and fulfilled if she does not have children or a family, and no matter how she justifies it, whether by saying that the world is already over-populated or that she doesn't make enough money to properly support a child. Having a great career is a great thing and I wish each woman or man who desires it to have one. But this is but an individual achievement, it is for you and you alone, (unless you spent much of your time and life truly helping others). Nothing you do for yourself can be as rewarding as something you do for others! Bringing life into the world and child-rearing are two of the most amazing creations possible; giving life to another is more gratifying than most things. I'm sure most women realize that when reaching a certain age. I'm also certain that most men realize that togetherness, love and sharing are much more important than a career life or a life more devoted to the 'one' rather than the 'two' or the family unit.

Aligned with the changes in recent decades and the now-accepted concepts of what it means to be a woman, something else has occurred. A lot of women equate staying at home and taking care of children with something demeaning. They feel that staying at home with a new-born is bowing to old-fashioned and chauvinistic thinking. Regarded in the past and by many women still today as a privilege and an extremely important part of raising a baby, nonetheless, more and more women nowadays consider any reference to staying at home, over and above the first few months, as humiliating, devaluing and indicative of patriarchy. Yet, we should consider and reconsider a couple of things: first, breast-feeding is exclusive to women, and the longer it is done the healthier the child will be. (Don't be fooled by doctors and their promises and statements about formulas. The quality of *any* formula does not even come near the quality of real mother's milk. There are quite a few *honest* and *objective* books and research papers on the subject.) Second, some men can indeed be amazing with children and even have as much patience for them as mothers do. But this is still the exception. This beautiful creature grew inside his mother's body for nine months; it was being fed, nourished and given oxygen and a safe environment by *her* to develop and evolve into a complete human being. And even after all that, the bond between the mother and the child is further strengthened by six, twelve and often more months of breast-feeding. The connection and closeness which exist between the two will probably be forever deeper than with the father. Men cannot, no matter how hard they try, manufacture that strong connection with the child. Furthermore, most likely due to all of the above, women possess maternal instincts which include being more sensitive to the child's needs and having a sense of great responsibility for it. This can be clearly seen even from a young age: girls are largely much more family-oriented than boys. The closeness between a mother and her child is in a way like being one person. The love accompanying this is almost always unequivocal or absolute.

This inherited ability to love their offspring wholly and unconditionally is possibly why women are capable of showing a similar love and devotion to men. Perhaps that is why they are also more romantic in nature.

A man can be an amazing parent or even be a better and warmer parent than the mother and have an awesome loving relationship with the child. But this does not take away from the fact that women have a fundamental, given and basic advantage over men in that respect from the beginning.

That second point is important because I'm of the opinion that, given this fundamental advantage women have, the child will benefit more from having his mother by his side for the first year or two – ideally of course would be to have both parents by the child's side, but that is rarely possible. The mother will have more patience with the child and will be better at raising it and will do so more naturally and with less effort. There are exceptions to every rule but in general this is true.

It is likely we could educate and train men to have more patience and better skills for raising children but I can't really see how we can close the gap on this enormous and innate advantage that a woman possesses of carrying the child in her womb for nine months, from conception through formation to its actual appearance: birth, in itself a powerfully bonding event.

The first years are of the highest importance to a new-born, to its family and society at large. Why not provide it with the absolute best possible conditions? Is being politically correct, a feminist or perhaps attempting fiercely to turn one's back on the ways of the past more important? Do we really think that giving all of the time possible and our best attention to a new-born makes us primitive again? That it means that we are back to being a chauvinistic and patriarchal society?

There are of course other factors related to this subject these days, especially when both parents have to work in order to provide for and support the family. Women, understandably, are reluctant to quit their jobs, cut short their careers and progress in life. In some countries there are very decent welfare conditions and laws supporting pregnant women, facilitating their period of pregnancy and the first year or two of the child's life; women receive financial support, they cannot be fired and can decide to return to work after a year or even two should they choose to. In other countries welfare conditions are not so generous. Society as a whole is not well-equipped to deal with this process fully.

Should we all, or most of us, revert to the belief and understanding that a child needs her/his mother by her/his side for the first year or two, I'm positive governments and laws will change and adapt accordingly.

Lifelong relationships

Older generations were wise to a few concepts our current generation apparently isn't. One of these is lifelong relationships and the appreciation of them. Even for those who still believe in the idea, it is extremely difficult these days to actually attain it.

For most of us, our first love is the strongest and most profound and we often look back at it with longing. It is not much of a proof for one thing or the other, but the intensity and veracity that first love (or the first two) embodies tell me that people would like to and are capable of falling in love and remaining in love. At the same time, in retrospect, many of us would dismiss or deprecate the first time we were in love. We would then say or think: "Oh how silly I was", "How young and innocent" or "I didn't know anything". These 'wisdoms' are mostly enforced upon us by the general state of society's and our own cynicism.

There are some remarkable and extremely gratifying rewards from lifelong relationships. Only when a person goes through one does he/she realize the truly profound and satisfying feelings and sense of accomplishment that can be had from it. Consider the feel-good factor and the self-gratifying feeling of standing by your word and being responsible for some minor matters such as being available and willing to help your parents or neighbours whenever they ask for it. Now, multiply that by a few score! That is how gratifying it is when one spends all of one's life in a responsible manner, respecting and fulfilling one's vows to one's spouse and children.

Even though in old age this gratifying feeling can be overshadowed by much of the regular stuff that old people can worry about or suffer from physically or mentally, the strong sense of honesty, dedication and devotion one has after adhering to these values all one's life is nonetheless ever-present, and this acts as a sturdy and comforting foundation on which one can rest.

These comforting emotions one has earned are also further supported and greatly magnified by the appreciation and respect given by loved ones and people around us who have been witnessing this mature and responsible behaviour from which they can also draw on and use as a good example. Not to mention the feeling of closeness that grows and the bond between the two and/or the family as a whole which deepens with each passing year. Overcoming obstacles, going through some tough times together and coming out successfully the other end make really strong connections between two people or a family. Nothing can come even remotely close to delivering such sensations of fulfilment and satisfaction. Only a long period of time spent well and honestly together can generate that.

It is not for nothing when one revisits love songs and romantic movies that one finds they all talk about falling in love and staying together forever, walking hand in hand into the sunset, living happily ever after. No love song talks about, "to be with you for a while and then with another" (until recently, that is, where we now find the odd one that does). There is something in us that longs for one, long, meaningful love and a life of faithfulness and dedication. We yearn for that purity. After all, these are values that we cherish. Not betrayal, cheap thrills and irresponsibility.

The feeling of satisfaction and gratification from spending a lifelong relationship with another person, seeing your children grow and having a family is incomparable to any modern concept, attitude or philosophy about relationships. As just mentioned, the dedication and devotion embraced and given through many a year cannot be equalled by any short-term type of thinking or action. Men, who generally need to accomplish much more in life than women in order to feel fulfilled, calm and satisfied in their twilight years, can come close to attaining that by being monogamous, building a family and respecting their wives and children throughout life. Earning real love and respect from people is an enormously rewarding thing. By being trustworthy, dedicated and devoted to one's spouse and children one will earn their honest love and respect and that will surely give a degree of comfort to anyone.

A family, a group of people bonded together, provides unconditional love and devotion. Only in a family can these things be obtained. The family unit is the only place where we can feel loved unconditionally and know that we won't be forgotten or neglected at the drop of a hat. Certainly, many families are far from perfect but still, in our society, great and true friends who will provide us with the loyalty that we all pine for are a rarity and this is much more likely to be found in the family unit. In a perfect world, which we are indeed capable of attaining, friendships could provide similar affection, love and trust.

Stability brings trust and trust in turn brings more stability. This means that the more stability we have, the more trust we will have as well. No existence can be considered sane, enjoyable or even reasonable without trust. From this we can infer that nothing can truly last in a constructive and gratifying manner without some stability.

In addition, when one pays positive attention to others, i.e. one's wife and children, one is much more likely to be more productive and happier in his/her personal life than if one were to focus his/her attention mainly on oneself. We feel a much bigger sense of calm and fulfilment when we give to, help and care for others, and as a result the tending to and caring for our own selves then become easier and smoother, our own problems seem smaller and less grave and we spend less time worrying about ourselves; we have others to think of as well and to be there for them. Besides, life can be trying and to get over all the hurdles, whether they be financial or emotional, is much more difficult to do alone than with a partner. Two people can overcome obstacles much faster and more smoothly than a single person can. Essentially a person feels much better, safer and more social when he/she receives love and affection from his/her parents and siblings but when that person has his/her own children and partner, not only does he/she feel these things but also, he/she grows to be a better, deeper, more caring and more responsible human being.

The most fundamental building block of our society is the family unit. A society can sustain a low percentage of unmarried people without any real damage to its fabric, but we are very close to crossing that line – if we haven't already. Were this institution to break down completely we would be facing massive changes in our lives and the lives of future generations. Changes for the worse in each and every respect.

Take juvenile delinquents and criminals for instance, a lot of them never had a real, loving or stable family. A big part of a person's perspectives about life and his/her consequent behaviour and attitudes towards life are based upon and influenced by his/her parents' characters and the way they raised him/her. Parents exert a tremendous influence upon a child which is in most cases positive.

By the way, a single mother or father does not constitute half a family, it is less. One parent cannot, nor does she/he hold the potential to, exert fifty percent of the influence that two parents can. When a family is comprised of both mother and father the child benefits from his mother separately, his father separately and from the influence of both parents being and acting together as a team, as a couple, which is an extra and a different thing again.

Affection is the single biggest impactful thing in our lives. When a child is growing up without enough of it, all of his/her perspectives on life will defer to what they would have been if he/she had been raised in a healthy family or simply had more affinity. A child growing up in a broken home, with a single mother or without enough affection will often become rougher and more cynical, alienation can set in and this will take its toll in many a shape and form. This process and its ramifications are very injurious to society at large.

For eons and eons, psychologically and biologically driven, the family unit has been the bedrock of society. That structural basis is imprinted on us, genetically, biologically and psychologically. Yes, a child can be raised by a single mother and be relatively happy and successful as an adult. Still, there will be fractures in his psyche and on an emotional level due to the reasons discussed above. Just because it has become almost the norm, it doesn't mean people no longer carry any emotional and psychological baggage with them when growing up in a single-parent home. Some may pretend as if they don't care and that it doesn't really matter, but they are indeed damaged to a degree.

Picture a boy of four. That boy, from the first moment he opened his eyes has had two loving people around him constantly. He has had the affection of two people. If these were relatively happy the affinity given was in abundance and engulfing. Now his parents are getting a divorce, this child, now and all of a sudden has one person to care, tend and be with him; the void created in a child's life, especially at a young age, is huge and most often cannot be filled. In addition, we should not forget how impactful and deleterious the process of getting a divorce and the consequent emotional states of both parents can be on the child, especially the emotional impact on the parent the child is left with.

We, as people, get damaged to an extent simply by going through and experiencing life with its ups and downs, peaks and valleys. We normally accept it and consider it to be part and parcel of the business of living. In addition, every so often big impacting changes occur in cultures and societies and there is not much we seem to be able to do about them but to accept them. We simply go on living, we must. We try to make the best of the situation. It's in our natures. The trouble is we also tend to quickly forget how things used to be only a short while before and we adapt rapidly to the new circumstances.

This simultaneously fortunate and unfortunate fact – that we always feel that we must keep going no matter what – makes it hard for us to take a step back, focus, observe, learn and understand the effects broken homes have on society. Yes, there are studies and research but they're neither read nor embraced by people. Only observations on a personal level could perhaps change a person's perspectives and attitudes. We'd all be better off taking the time to dwell on that subject, trying to understand and realize its ramifications for us personally, our children and grandchildren and for society as a whole.

When a child innately and naturally expects two parents and then gets only one, it has consequences. And don't think for a second we can get used to that either. Even if each and every family unit were broken up right now and that situation were to continue for another fifteen generations, children of the generation after would still suffer a loss, feel hurt and sense that something is missing growing up with only one parent. The two-parent mould is imprinted on us. Look at our bodies, physics, our biology, genders…

When a child grows up with no parents at all, the situation is obviously much graver. Within the family unit close connections, protection, love, respect and appreciation are much more in abundance than society at large, where most people are relative strangers to the child.

Attraction

Let us turn our attention to a very basic thing without which relationships would not be so exciting and desired: attraction.

What is attraction? Why is it at all possible for us to be attracted to others? What are the powers at work here?

Attraction is the feeling of wanting to be physically close to someone else. Physical attraction is closely related to the desire to have sex but is not the same thing. I believe the subject can be broken down into three main factors or reasons. The first factor is the same one responsible for our desire for sex: the natural and basic biological draw between people to have sex, reproduce, procreate.

Second: attraction is possible where differences exist, mainly biological and physical ones. We can't be attracted to ourselves, really. We are attracted to another person, a different being.

Let's say two people are different to one another spiritually, yet their bodies, demeanour and behaviour are exactly the same. For them to find each other attractive would be a real stretch, almost impossible. But when we begin to introduce some biological or physical distinctions: different looks or demeanour, namely, attraction becomes plausible and we can complement each other. Two of the same do not match or work in this universe. Everything in the biological, chemical and physical worlds seeks to be complemented by another or something else. Like our bodies, only two different sexes can create a new-born. In chemistry, all the elements responsible for each and every form in the world and possibly the universe are looking to join others to be able to fully achieve a result or work to the fullest extent of their potential.

The more distinctions we introduce, the more plausible it is for us to feel attraction to another, yet on a mental and behavioural level the two have to have some things in common. They would have to share some resemblance in character, goals and perspectives. A bit of common ground is needed in order to work together as a couple, as a team.

The third factor: the mental or spiritual connection we feel with another or the affection we have for another's mental or spiritual disposition. This can be called mental or spiritual attraction. This kind of attraction can be strictly on a platonic level – like the affinity we are able to feel towards those whom we share things in common, find interesting, who can exert a positive influence on our lives or who are simply funny and amusing. But when we feel a connection with or mental affection for a person from the opposite sex *stronger* than a basic one, often and instinctively that mental attraction can be transformed into a physical one as well. One of the main reasons this happens is because we all love to show affection, and the way we normally do so in this tangible/physical world is mostly through physical closeness: touching, hugging and more. We live inside of and through the body; almost everything we do is manifested by physical actions. Thus, when we feel a strong mental attraction, the desire to express it physically may arise. That is why we can, and often do, very easily cross the fine line between mental attraction or closeness to someone into also desiring them physically. This happens to men more than it does to women. Women are normally excellent at keeping things strictly on a platonic, mental level. And when they do feel a stronger affection and connection to someone they know better how to stop those feelings from overflowing and crossing the line.

These three factors: biology, differences and mental/spiritual attraction working interrelatedly, serve to determine our individual tastes and preferences and the degrees of attraction we feel.

In most cases, the better and closer spiritual connection two people have, the more likely they are to cross the line into the realm of physical attraction as well. It rarely works the other way around – when physical attraction or the act of sex 'encourages' one to be spiritually closer to another. Except, sometimes it does; in my opinion strictly due to the actual physical *closeness* of the two; the act of being near one another and not due to the sexual attraction or the act of sex itself. Closeness will automatically make people feel close and that can encourage them to take more interest in one another.

Due to all of the above, it only makes sense then that the emotions of affinity, closeness or affection can all be confused with the emotions of intimacy and sexual desire. Women know this well, and from a young age too. They know that men (it happens to women too, but less) can often confuse or misconstrue a smile, a hug or a nice conversation and think that they actually desire them or have something sexual in mind. Which is why many women stay away from, or try to avoid getting too close to, men – even if only on mental or spiritual levels. Most women, as opposed to many men, keep their intimate thoughts and sexual desires in check and to themselves or for time spent privately with their boyfriends or husbands. They don't normally transmit these while walking down the street, looking at someone or when engaging in a conversation.

Attraction and memories

Our tastes, preferences, wants, desires and decisions can also be affected and altered by our past experiences; memories which hold in them the experience, knowledge, concepts and ideas we have accumulated during our lives. These can control or at least influence the way we act and behave. Past experiences can, and do to a degree, direct, lead, encourage or dissuade us with regard to anything we do. As an example: if a girl had a bad experience with a boy she used to date when she was young, then later, boys who resembled him in any shape or form might trigger something in her and likely to make her become somewhat prejudiced toward them. It is very likely that she would have apprehensions about dating a boy of this sort, but at the same time she could also be specifically looking to go out with such boys. There exists a particular subconscious mechanism which can sometimes kick in: the desire to *please* someone who hurt you, endangered you or was very displeased with you.

Thus, every choice or decision we make, and the things we like or dislike, are all, to one degree or another, also shaped or reshaped by our past experiences. To what extent? Well, that depends on the person and her/his experience (all past memories) and the degree to which that experience influences her/him.

Attraction and control

We would all generally prefer to be logical people and in control of our lives. I don"t mean to suggest, though, that when it comes to sex and attraction it would be better for us to be able to decide completely and utterly who we are attracted to, the level of attraction and when and where. That would be cold and robotic – something we all try to stay away from as much as possible. But on the opposite side to complete control exists a condition whereby we let ourselves go and surrender almost all of our control to urges and bodily needs, letting them lead us and thus becoming much less selective regarding whom we find attractive, are attracted to, to what degree and when.

These two opposite extremes are both undesirable conditions. Hence, to be in a condition where we are capable of somewhat spontaneously feeling attraction is good and needed. In order to assume and remain in that condition, we need to exert some degree of control and be logical and tactful as well.

It would be great if men could embrace the more humane approach that most women still possess – when a woman looks at a man to whom she feels attraction, in the vast majority of cases the attraction she is feeling and projecting is more a desire for intimacy than lust and a strictly sexual urge. Women search for intimacy primarily. Were that to be the case with men, the whole subject of attraction would be less problematic and we would be facing a problem of a smaller magnitude.

There is no issue, on the contrary, with letting ourselves go when it comes to spiritual attraction. This will do us only good. It will generate more friendship, warmth and affinity in our lives. All of us could use more innocent and productive human interactions.

The dangers of some emotions

Biology: bodies can generate powerful emotions, sex probably being the most powerful of them all. No wonder people like Freud and others have dedicated so much to sex in their research and writings. It is a major button for us all. Generally, we are all suckers for feelings, meaning that we love to feel. It is what makes us human. We feel so alive when we feel. We would even prefer to feel depressed, down or sad than to not feel anything at all. We basically live to feel. And when we feel we naturally want to continue feeling, have more of it. Hence it is easy to get sucked in by powerful emotions.

Attraction between two people who have never met before can be very strong. We all know what emotions beginnings can generate. Especially in men – women are less likely to let matters get out of hand or be lost in the whirl of these strong emotions. Normally, during the very early stages of the relationship, women control their emotions rationally and look at the big picture, considering the viability and the chances of success the relationship they are about to enter into holds. Women are aware of these potentially powerful emotions and the perils of physical attraction; therefore, they know better and in general stay away from unnecessary closeness to men. They are familiar with the effect it can have on them and aware of the fact that under the influence of these emotions people find it difficult to think straight and often make mistakes they usually regret soon after.

It's under our control

As a prerequisite to having the desire to have sex or any sexual contact, one has to permit oneself to feel that desire – to be attracted to someone else. In general, even though we all have strong biological urges pulling and pushing us, we must first ALLOW ourselves to feel attraction in order to be attracted. Feeling attracted to someone is mostly a choice. Women know that. This is easiest to see with a woman who is in love and happy with her boyfriend: she's not looking for anything else or thinking about anyone else, but as soon as it is over and she's available she allows herself to feel attracted to new people, she is 'on the market' again. Women, much more than men, can control whom they feel attraction to, when and where – or at least stifle it when it creeps up on them. But even men, when they are in love or excited about the girl whom they are with, don't allow themselves to look at other girls or get attracted to them as easily as they would do when single.

Each and every one of us can look at somebody and decide whether to be attracted to that person or not, it is a choice. Indeed, at times it can be difficult to control – our level of control depends on our mental state, level of contentment in life and other factors, but it is always more of a choice than not.

It is often troubling to a man to witness how easily a woman can shut off and not feel attraction when she so decides. Whether it's while making out, already naked in bed prior to the act or even during the act itself.

Yet, of late, both men and women have been allowing themselves to feel attraction to others more easily and less discriminately. Many are letting their sexual wants and needs dictate to them more than the other way around. These days, much more than in the past, we can see and progressively feel the mental and physical sexual insinuations and innuendos thrown in all directions with little thought for the consequences, anywhere from clubs, bars and cafés to the workplace. It feels as though more and more people have decided to move away from control, choice and sensible decisions with regards to sex and attraction and allow themselves to feel attraction to whomever fits their ever-broadening and loosening standards; to let themselves go. Once commenced and practiced for a while it is then not simple to stop. As a result, many today, even when in a relationship, allow themselves (or simply have become ok, used to or comfortable with the idea) to feel attraction to other people as well.

By allowing this to go on even further, usually incrementally, cheating may occur and then its inevitable consequences: broken trust, break-ups, divorce, broken homes, single-parent households, loneliness. Men and women should seriously consider the ramifications of their actions before plunging into irresponsibility.

One unspoken and quite hidden aspect of this subject is that sexual attraction aimed and directed at someone is, in most instances, a type of request, an ask, the posing of a question. When you are attracted to someone – in her/his presence that is – it is as if you are very subtly and to an extent asking something of that person, that you are expecting or wishing for something. By having intimate and personal thoughts about her/him you are essentially projecting an interest which is directed at that person. That person senses it and to her/him it feels like you desire something of her/him, as if you're asking, waiting or expecting a reply in a way. This can, and often does, make people uncomfortable.

A platonic relationship or a simple interaction between two people would take on a different complexion and the quality of it would reduce if one of the two begins to project his/her desire to get something from the other while the other doesn't want to give it or be part of it. Whether it be sex or anything else.

Most people would like to lead their lives and daily routines without having to have these sexual thoughts and wants thrown at them. Most, especially women, would like to be treated, talked to and interacted with without them being stripped naked in the thoughts and mind of the person opposite them. Most people would prefer an innocent and honest interaction. Otherwise what is it all for? Interactions? Conversations? Friendships? Are they only there in order for us to potentially get together and use each other's bodies to satisfy our needs?

Quite a few people, again predominantly women, when they are flirting or showing and projecting some interest or sexuality, do *not* necessarily do so with the intention of going any further than flirting or further than the mere entertainment of ideas about sex and sexual encounters. Yet even this reduces the general level and quality of human interactions. An innocent interaction free of sexual innuendo or thoughts is a human interaction between the souls, between the substance, logic and reason of the people involved. Any time sex or intimate interest enter the equation the whole thing is reduced in quality, often to a fairly cheap interaction. Men! You will not be scoring many points with women in such fashion, much less than you would were you to behave asexually and converse innocently until such time when sexual innuendo and behaviour is merited. Women respect and respond very positively to that kind of behaviour.

It goes without saying that by letting ourselves feel attraction more easily and less discriminately to others, we promote a form of emotional instability from which we will all suffer. This will mean an even greater confusion between men and women than that which already exists. Previous decades and centuries were broadly more innocent – no matter how perverse a culture was, most of its perversions were normally kept out of the public eye and done in secret. Therefore, interactions were more innocent and honest. This maintained a semblance of sanity in society and this in turn kept some of people's sexual urges and wants in check.

That issue of unchecked attraction may sound like a minor or trivial thing but it is a fairly big matter when one cares to look at it from a broader perspective. Unchecked and wild, it can deliver quite a blow to the foundations of any potentially sane society; foundations which are comprised of the innocent desire to live together and share life and things of trust and substance.

Sublimation

There exists a term in the English language which I'm rather fond of, and that is 'sublimation'. I like the way the word sounds, but mostly I like what it means. 'Sublimation' is basically transforming an undesired emotion or urge into a desired and positive one instead. Feelings and emotions (used here interchangeably) are the most valuable commodities in life, and life without them can hardly be called life. Yet, we are all aware that at the same time emotions can also be painful, burdensome and controlling. We don't generally like these kinds of emotions and often try to avoid them or get rid of them when they encroach upon us. An urge is also a type of emotion. One of the strongest urges we all possess, talked about at length in this book, is the sexual urge. Although it is stronger and more accentuated in men – women are less influenced by sex drives and more prudent in attitude – it is nonetheless shared by women. We are also all aware how society in recent times has been subjected to more and more sex stimuli and manipulation due to the openness about the subject and the emphasis placed upon it.

When one can resist a particular urge or an emotion which one does not want to act upon or be controlled by, and then diverts that drive or urge into doing something constructive instead, one is said to be exercising sublimation. Artists, in particular, are familiar with this mechanism and go through it often; sublimating (substituting) the urge to have sex, to drink or to do anything which they deem unconstructive with creativity; doing something creative like writing, composing, painting, etc... Were that concept of sublimation advocated for and promoted in society, appreciated more and regarded as an ability to aspire to, more people would be able to sublimate their controlling or somewhat destructive urges and emotions with constructive ones for the benefit of themselves and the people around them.

Modesty and
past perceptions

People today generally practice less modesty in their mode of dress and comportment than in most of recorded history.

Modesty is a relative term, but it is coined and embraced in similar ways and has had similar meanings in most cultures.

The definition of modesty was conceived based on the 'buttons' people have with regards to sex and attraction, and in accordance with the extent to which their emotions and urges can be provoked by the pressing of these buttons. In other words, a modest dress code would mean covering enough of one's body in order not to easily or strongly evoke sexual thoughts and desires in the observer. We are all pretty much aware of people's buttons; we know what can evoke sexual thoughts or emotions in us and most likely in another. There is a line that can generally be drawn based on this knowledge. When a person doesn't cross that line, that person could be said to be relatively modest in her/his way of dressing and comportment. This line has been pushed further and further back in recent decades.

Sexy is sexier to us when our imaginations are called into action. Women know that very well, of course, and usually have that knowledge down to a T. In my opinion, women don't have to try hard to be sexy, like dressing or comporting themselves in a provocative manner, in order to elicit a response from men. All that's required of them is to be aesthetic; dress in a feminine way; indeed, be feminine, that will do the trick. Men's imaginations are active enough as they are and not much is required to get them going.

Depiction and image

It is neither easy nor simple to be a woman or a man these days. People with power and in high and key positions often use their influence – whether it be through the media and/or other means – to attempt to change the minds of people (often successfully) with regard to themselves; the way they think, behave and ultimately who they are. This has always been the case but today, with the long and overreaching arm of the world-wide-web, their influence is magnified tenfold. The music and movie industries, and the media in general, increasingly and blatantly depict a woman as a strong person physically, a force to be reckoned with, someone who can be as violent as a man, someone who takes the initiative when it comes to sex and courtship and even takes the man"s traditional job in the actual act of sex (which is not to say, of course, that a woman should only lie there on her back and do nothing). They call it female empowerment. That kind of 'empowerment' can only happen in the minds of people who believe that physical strength, violence and roughness are better than grace, class and elegance or in the minds of people who purposely try to blur the line between men and women. As far as I can gather, most women don't think like that, nor they would like the line to be blurred or disappear altogether. These depictions, then, generate confusion and shake the foundations most people used to operate on. Consequently, people are becoming unstable, along with the family unit, the marriage institution and relationships in general.

If, as a woman, you want to be that way and you think that this is the best way for you, I humbly say, go ahead and be what you want to be. I believe this is the most important thing: to be whom you want to be. Yet, I'm pretty sure most women would like to remain the gentle (and gentle does not mean weak), feminine creatures they are. The VAST majority of women don't seem to care for fighting crime and jumping out of buildings or about being as strong as a man, nor about being the 'man' in bed. Most want to be treated with respect, in a gentlemanly way, to be given equal rights and opportunities, and not to be harassed and treated as a sex object.

Which women do you think have the ascendancy; who are sending and spreading the more positively influential vibes and energy toward others and the environment, and are also more appreciated and desired? Those depicted recently in the media who are fighting crime like a man, sleeping with many partners, treating sex only as a means to satisfy their urges and reacting aggressively and in a rough manner to anyone who says anything unkind to her? Or women like Lisa from 'Rear Window', Sabrina from 'Sabrina', Sandy from 'Grease' or Jo Ann from 'Tequila Sunrise'?

In my eyes there is no comparison! The new style of woman depicted and made out to be like a man in almost every way is nowhere near the level and quality of image women normally had up until fifteen, twenty or thirty years ago: fundamentally *different* to that of a man. Women were what they are, feminine, desired as such and on a slightly higher plane than men!

Reacting – replying aggressively and in a rough manner to comments, slurs and anything derogatory towards them – is a theme that of late has been pushed and promoted in certain media. It is rare to find a classic, graceful reaction from a woman on such platforms these days. This is portrayed as a cool thing: don't be a victim, react strongly, use swear words, abusive tones and language, react like men, don't be a push-over, don't remain silent, talk back, be a strong woman and other such attitudes. Since when is matching your abuser in tone and language a virtue? Don't we all have more respect for a person who keeps a cool head and behaves maturely by NOT stooping to the same level as her/his abuser? Sure, there is the need and desire to no longer be treated as a second-rate human. Women have had enough and they would like to be treated nicely and respectfully. But that feeling of retaliation which comes from anger and bitterness is not a virtuous one; nor is it shared by most women, who habitually prefer to be cordial, nice and softly-spoken. Still, the talk-back-matching-your-abuser culture which is being promoted by a small number of people influences many and serves to further alienate women from men.

Yes, we can find more and more guys today who find it sexy when a woman beats a man to a pulp or jumps out of a burning building or when she behaves like a man in bed. People's minds can be conditioned to accept anything! Create enough movies portraying women who do these things as sexy, shove it in people's faces long enough and some will be conditioned, there's no doubt. But I'm pretty sure that that will fairly quickly get old and that *living* with such a woman won't be as thrilling or productive as some might initially think.

Old-fashioned ideas are not some distant history or ancient concepts. There are still lots and lots of women who think like that, in the 'old-fashioned way'. We need only help it back up from beneath the surface of this new, pervasive and, in a way, enforced social veneer.

Possible future

It might not seem so, but we determine our own futures. We are responsible for everything which happens to us and in the world in general, even though many turns of events or occurrences may appear accidental, consequential or simple luck. It's true that the powers-that-be can and do influence our lives, and to one degree or another control our destinies, whether it be through economic policies or otherwise. Still, when we examine the pages of history we come across many examples of individuals rising above great difficulties and hardship to accomplish what had hitherto seemed impossible. We can then truly comprehend the power of the one, as well as discovering that most, if not all, of the positive changes and progress through history in every field or subject were conceived or initiated by one person. One person can change the world! Thus, not only can a person control her/his own destiny but other's as well. This is not a cliché. It is a claim backed by many instances throughout history proving its veracity. It is all about belief, conviction and perseverance. You lead, others will follow and a change will come.

That being said, I don't believe that each of us is obliged to have millions of followers, though: simply by controlling one's destiny and by setting a good example, one will have assisted her/his loved ones in controlling theirs, in this way the world could instantly be changed for the better.

At the moment society is sliding down a slippery slope regarding the fundamental subjects of relationships and femininity. These are vast subjects with many possible implications. When a person has never felt the true love of a spouse and a child, his/her fundamental perceptions on friendships and relationships in general won't be as positive, productive or warm as they could be. His/her sense of community and social awareness won't be as high as it could be, either.

If you see this in the same way as I do, you have the power to do something about it – you really do! By not going along with things you don't agree with and also by speaking out against matters and practices you believe should cease or be restrained, you can start a trend or at least slow the decline. It is not as difficult as you think it is. Many have already begun to rise up and give voice to their opinions and desires for change with regard to these and other subjects discussed in this book. One thing we can all easily do right away is take a step back, look ahead into the future and picture our culture, our society five, ten or thirty years from now – and if we don't like what we see we can then start doing things aimed at obtaining a different and better outcome.

For me, femininity is a human art form, the human manifestation of art. I would like to see it regarded and appreciated the way it was in the past. I believe femininity is vitally important for maintaining equilibrium between the genders, an equilibrium based on differences. To me, a world without femininity, grace or class would be a cold world, a world where the two genders are almost identical, a confused world, one which is largely sex-oriented, less spiritual, rougher and with much less beauty in it.

Do we really want a woman to carry a man across the threshold on their wedding night or lift a refrigerator up the stairs? What would we be achieving by that?

Would carrying a man across the threshold make a woman feel good about herself? Would she feel more equal then? Stronger? Quite a few women today would like to see it happen, but I'm happily convinced that most would not. I strongly believe that the quest for that kind of 'equality' stems from the misconception and confusion on the part of many women today who think that doing things that men do and in the way men do somehow makes them more equal. Up until approximately twenty-five years ago a woman wanted to be treated like one, in a gentlemanly fashion. Gentlemanliness was considered the gold standard of attitudes. Women knew better. They knew that being carried across the threshold is higher on the chart of human interactions than being the carrier. It is simple logic, but today in many a place it's being twisted and turned on its head.

Our basic natures

People are basically good – I strongly believe that to be true, otherwise why would we have the international bill of human rights, courts which primarily seek justice, ethics watchdog committees in almost every major body or organization and a population of which the vast majority (some 97-98 percent) believes that hurting another human being is wrong and would not condone it.

Clearly, many parts and members of the institutes mentioned above are corrupt and are far from being just or fair, or administer real justice. But the fact that we have these institutions in the first place and that we all agree they should exist goes to show that most of us expect and seek fairness, justice and protection from unjust harm and evildoers.

Good people can also do bad things, which is why it is very hard to maintain the belief that people are basically good. It is extremely hard to do so for instance when your spouse has just told you he has been cheating and lying to you for the last two years. The subject of goodness and badness can thus be very bewildering.

It is very interesting that the more a person individuates or internalizes, the more that person will think primarily about himself and thus be more liable to act selfishly and hurt others inadvertently or even deliberately. He would therefore become more 'bad'.

The more individualistic we become, the more difficult it is for us to live in a group, a team or, more pertinent to the subjects of this book, have a successful relationship. Togetherness is all about you and I, she and him. It's about finding common ground, some compromise, working things out, overcoming arduous times together, neither giving up nor giving in easily and quickly, even if it means some sacrifice. It is all for the benefit of the two, of the family, the future. These, in turn benefit the individual on an individual level as well.

Hence when one's life is not only about oneself but a lot about others as well, one will find it easier to express and exhibit one's better self and one's positive sides and to be good. The more time a person spends caring for and thinking of others the more he/she will understand and have empathy for others and therefore be less liable to hurt them. *'Togetherness' makes better people.*

Combining the two together

There was evidently a purpose in the creation. No matter who and what created our bodies, they were created to complement one another and by that to reach some level of harmony. There is not much to life without the striving and the potential for harmony. Everything under the sun and above is complemented by something else. Each and all exist thanks to something else which in turn exists thanks to another thing and so it goes.

The differences in our bodies are there for a purpose, they make life interesting and challenging. Life without challenges can hardly be lived and will probably end badly in depression for all. Picture a reality whereby all our bodies are the same, all can create life and the babies that are being born are able to self-sustain right away or within a very short time. This would mean no togetherness or parenthood are necessary. Life would then be much less interesting, to say the least.

When a woman is asking her husband to help her with the shopping bags, to reach higher to the top kitchen cupboard or to move the sofa, she is manifesting the symbiotic relationship they have; she needs him for some things, he needs her for others. The creation of two different genders who only TOGETHER can create life, their different bodies' muscle composition and different bodily systems are responsible for the fundamental need for the symbiotic, challenging and interesting relations between them. The differences between the sexes are manifested in their physical appearances and behaviour as well. We can also look at the subject of the two sexes complementing one another from another angle, a more poetic and romantic one.

Everything we build and all that exists have a foundation: a strong base and a finish – an aesthetic or not so aesthetic one, whether it be a building, a bridge, a tree, a hill or a pen. Looking at something we understandably notice the outside first; it can be beautiful, nice or simply plain. But upon contemplation, if we choose to investigate further, we realize the strength of it or its build, its foundation. That could be a good old-fashioned analogy of men and women, working in synergy, complementing one another.

Obviously, women can be both strong, with a great foundation, as well as pretty and aesthetic, just as can men be gentle, aesthetic, handsome and strong as well. Even though women are usually the ones who provide more of the *mental* foundation for the relationship, in terms of biology and physics the analogy generally works, men are more creatures of muscles and strength and women are more of beauty and tenderness.

Strength and force are impressive, they play a big part in life and are needed, obviously. They can also be very inspiring and impactful. Still, in most matters in life they cannot accomplish what gentleness and elegance can.

Which do you think is more powerful, a pretty flower or a screwdriver?

A beautiful picture or a rock?

gentleness or roughness?

Which has a more positive influence over people or humanity?

Of course, both the flower and the screwdriver – having different roles in life – are needed and can be equally useful. A screwdriver is very valuable and can evidently do things that a flower cannot. Women can be strong and do most things that men can, but it is unnecessary for them, in my opinion, to put in effort to try to be as strong as men or like men; they possess other features as we have already seen, and these are even more supreme to those of men. The screwdriver, analogous to a man of course, can also possess charm and an aesthetic finish all while being very useful and appreciated. Still, very few people would stop to admire one in a shop window – unless it were *really* special. It won't generally be marvelled at; neither watched nor put on display in a room as decoration. Yet most people would appreciate the beauty of a flower or a statue in passing. Women are the living decoration of this world!!

People are more complex, clearly, and some men can be impressive enough to be marvelled at, but I believe this analogy is still applicable.

Take a second to think about the impact women have on this world. Imagine a world without the female form! It is like nature with no flowers, trees and green grass.

Femininity and the pursuit of women comprise one of the few major endeavours of men in life, which I believe are: self-accomplishment and money (power and position), family and women. In what order, I'll let you decide for yourself. But I can assure you, eliminating the pursuit, attainment and retainment of women from the equation would make life for men extremely dull.

Virtual world

The virtual world is a major contributing factor to the changes in cultures and societies in recent times. The more time we spend in the virtual world, the less time we spend in real life and the more we become individuated, which at the end of the day means loneliness – regardless of the number of virtual friends one has. This is the main and most deleterious effect that that world exerts upon us.

Things change and move very rapidly in this world. After a while this will reduce a person's (any person's) ability to focus, pay attention and concentrate. There, images, pages or subjects move and change faster than things do in real life. When we spend a lot of time on virtual media we get used to the higher speed at which things happen there. Upon returning to reality things may then appear and feel too slow for us. As a result, we become impatient and unable to focus for long periods of time; we become restless. (The average attention span of young people has been dramatically reduced of late.)

Virtual media naturally place the emphasis on the visual side of things, i.e. photos and videos. This, combined with the care-of-the-body-culture which has been centre stage in western cultures for a long while now, has been pushing people deeper into a state of mind in which looks and appearance are extremely important, revered and admired. More and more people care more about the way they look and the way others do, too.

In addition, after spending years consumed by photos and videos, life through the eyes of a camera then becomes the reality preferred and courted by many; a type of life which principally is not in concert with reality. Things in real life are more difficult, neither as easy nor as smooth as depicted in a still photo or a video. People in photos and videos look happy, contented, larger than life and their lives seem cool and groovy in most cases. That kind of portrayed reality is usually better than the life the average person normally leads, thus making one wish he/she had had a better life, a life as cool and easy-going as those people on the screen have. This makes one disregard or devalue one's own life to a greater or lesser extent. These desirable but mostly unreal 'realities' drive a wedge between us and real-life situations and real people, rendering us more and more incapable of coping with and accepting real life.

Another aspect of the passive-observer role we assume when spending time on virtual media is the pushing of oneself further and further inside one's head. While we are observing and watching in the virtual world we are mostly inside our heads, in our own world; thinking, trying to understand, imagining and picturing scenarios and situations. That is living in a rather more theoretical or virtual world than a practical or real one. When one does so long enough one is then 'pushed' *out* of the present (present time); naturally one then keeps less and less contact with the immediate things, people or environment, therefore one becomes less aware of them. It is like when we look directly at something but our thoughts are elsewhere; we aren't really seeing, hearing or in real contact with that thing, like when we daydream. Most don't become that detached, obviously, nevertheless we all become less and less present. Picture that happening a number of times a day or for minutes upon minutes or even hours during the day for someone; this person's ability to be present, focus and concentrate in real life, to be efficient and handle things, will obviously reduce.

The trouble is, most people don't notice themselves becoming less and less present (in full contact with the environment) and therefore become less alert and less present to a marked degree before they or anyone else even notices. By that time, it is normally very difficult for one to revert and better his/her condition; one's habits, routines and affection for social media or the virtual world in general are difficult to fight or change.

Moreover, and very importantly, the virtual world inevitably paints and builds an image inside us of how life could and should be, how relationships should be (for example, pictures of happy couples and short happy videos). As it happens, when we run into trouble in a relationship and it no longer fits the image we have in our heads of how cool, easy and smooth life and relationships should be, compounded by the fact that we have been living in a more theoretical world rather than a practical one and have thus lost some of our ability to cope with what's real, we give up with barely a fight. Many today don't possess the nerve to even try to start a relationship nor the optimism that it would work. Real life has become too real for us, too hard to handle.

Relationships, aspects of and tips for

We live for and love interaction. Simple, every day or casual interactions between people are easy to manage and enjoy; however, when an interaction becomes more personal and intimate, things can get a little more complicated. In a close relationship we share intimate information and we are more exposed as people on every level: mental, emotional and physical. Due to the strong feelings involved and the degree of closeness, we can find ourselves acting and behaving in ways we never thought we could or never believed possible for us. The reactions and behaviours which intense emotions can evoke are on a whole different level and can at times make a person feel like or seem to be like a different person altogether. The level and intensity of feelings like anger, upset, confusion and discontent are relative to the positive emotions we feel for one another. The more we love one another the more disconcerting a fight or a crisis is for us. This is one of the main reasons why we can at times find ourselves lost, hopeless and helpless facing various situations in a relationship.

We study for almost everything in life. We are expected to have a degree from college or university in order to get a good job and to be certified or have the relevant experience for nearly anything that requires knowledge and responsibility to do or operate. Yet, for having a relationship, a child and a family there are no specific requirements. We are expected to know all there is to know about it and simply make it work. True, we are equipped with some basic knowledge about people and how to behave in or handle casual interactions. We are familiar with our own and also other people's run-of-the-mill emotional responses and reactions, as well as with some other aspects of common interrelations or regular friendships. Most of us have our parents as examples and a source of knowledge to draw on but they, like us, never had lessons on how to be in a relationship, and thus more often than not bestow upon us their own subjective interpretations and frustrations alike. Therefore, our partial, basic knowhow and the often-confusing impressions we pick up from our parents and the environment are rarely enough to make us confident and fully capable of maintaining a long and successful relationship or a family without running into difficulties.

There are a few fundamental elements to the subject of relationships that I believe if adhered to or nurtured will make any relationship better and successful. But before we dive into those I'd like to talk with you about your inner world.

Our inner worlds

The more a person objectively observes the environment and people, the more emotionally intelligent and wiser that person will be. That person will generally have more awareness. When one is able do so one is then more able to also observe oneself from the outside, meaning more objectively. This is very helpful and therapeutic. The more we are able to examine our lives from a different perspective to the one we constantly have – from within – the more objective we will be and as a result more capable and successful in everything we do in life. Seeing things from the outside is very educational. To do so one must be brave, though, because often we do not like what we see. Whether it's because it reminds us that we're not actually doing well, that we're not really achieving what we set out to achieve in our dreams and plans or just because it will be too hard to change course right now. Thus, we ordinarily prefer to remain inside ourselves and keep looking at things from the one perspective we know best: from inside our heads.

Due to the fragile composition of marriages and relationships these days, having the ability to look at things through a broader lens, with greater perspective, becomes even more significant.

One thing we can all easily do is to try and picture ourselves at fifty, sixty or seventy years of age after having lived life in a couple or more different ways. In line with the common practice in this day and age of staying single or being divorced, we can then picture ourselves at seventy after having lived a fully indulged life, having all the pleasures one can have with little or no accountability, not having produced anything long-lasting or stable like a marriage, a family or being there for our children – if we had any. How do you think you'd feel then? What would your general emotional state and your level of contentment and satisfaction be like, do you reckon? Would you regret not having done better or more? In comparison, we can picture a scenario whereby we have lived a life of love, responsibility and dedication to our loved ones; how do you think you'd feel then? Which scenario do you believe would count and mean more to you and your close ones? Which would give you more pride and satisfaction?

Most of us of course prefer 'togetherness' over 'alone'; married over divorced; and actually raising our children over not really being there when they grow up. Yet more and more people do less and less in order to keep their marriages alive, while at the same time fan the flames of their personal desires and wants at the expense of the family or the relationship.

We have all been to an extent victims of individuation (thinking more of ourselves, internalizing) in recent times and we need to understand the ramifications involved. We should realize the effect this process has on our ability to remain objective or see the big picture. One of the main drawbacks of this process is that when people become more individuated they generally become more emotional! When you, yourself, is the centre of your world, your main concern, your emotions, automatically become more apparent to you, you notice them more, they play a bigger role in your life. By taking a more important and central part in your life they then get to influence your thinking processes more and more. Thus, making you less and less able to be objective (see and understand the other person), cool-headed or composed. Emotions and feelings are not objective. We all know how difficult it is to remain objective and collected when filled with emotions.

Therefore, the more a person's inner world becomes the centre of his/her life (individuation), the less able will he/she be to truly interact with and understand others. In order to understand others well and consequently have better and deeper interactions with them, one needs to be able to look at and observe others objectively and dispassionately as much as one can. One has to be able to put oneself in another person's shoes, in place of another, to be able to be empathetic. These abilities are extremely important when trying to live with another or in a close group.

Normally, mere interaction with people, seeing them react, reason and express emotions, will give a person a better knowledge of them. Meaning, the more one interacts the better one will be at interacting. But that is only possible when one is still more objective than one is self-centred; before one goes inwards too deeply. When we are young we have a better shot at achieving that – the older we get the more individuated we are. These days, alas, people interiorize at a very young age.

When a person is constantly being fed his own emotions, his mind, ideas, opinions and concepts change accordingly and to varying degrees; to a marked degree in most cases. As a result, that person will find it terribly difficult to be able to listen, judge and adjudicate matters with a clear and objective mind, especially in matters concerning people who are close to him/her (fights with loved ones or parents for instance). In actuality, the person himself won't realize that he/she is not being objective; that person will be convinced of his/her own righteousness – after all, his/her emotions and experience tell him/her so.

Today, the ability to remain objective and dispassionate is more crucial than ever before. The process of becoming more and more individuated, of us living in our own worlds, is supported by and pushed on us from every corner, whether it be the media, our environment or technology. To overcome obstacles and tough times in relationships or life in general, and to resist all that's out there which can negatively influence us, one requires objectivity and the ability to have and maintain a broader perspective of life. Remaining relatively extroverted and objective we can then achieve more success regarding relationships and family.

Concerning relationships, each time we embark on a new one we are naturally older and arguably (and hopefully) more mature, so we feel that we are better equipped to handle it this time; after all, we know more, have more experience and have also learnt from our past mistakes. All of us are inclined to think that experience helps us, teaches us lessons, betters our decision-making processes and makes us more mature, responsible and objective. This is true to some extent, but for only *some* aspects of experience. How, though, would a bad experience like finding out about a betrayal, a big fight or memories of a break-up or a divorce, better your life, make you wiser and provide you with a broader perspective on life? By the time you enter, let's say your third relationship, you will have gained experience from your first and second ones and you will automatically draw on that experience and maybe do better this time regarding some (only some) aspects of the relationship. But let's say your third, fourth and fifth ones also fail. In that case you will no longer be able to draw on these experiences in a constructive manner or learn positive lessons for the future. You will simply get more confused about the subject and all its compartments and become more introverted (less able to be objective). The recollections of fights, heartaches and heartbreaks, and especially the break-ups, combined with the too-often disregarded and underrated knowledge that we didn't succeed in keeping the previous relationship together, will overshadow the good experience we have collected. The amount of confusion will rise in direct proportion to the number of times you enter into a new relationship.

We get touchier, more sensitive and less trusting after each broken relationship. Like, for example, when a man, in his third serious relationship, is faced with a situation whereby his wife returns home late one night after he'd been waiting up, not knowing where she was. The more time passes and the more he waits, the more a past memory of his starts to kick in: his first girlfriend coming home late several times and on the tenth occasion, while having an argument, it turned out that she was seeing someone else. This being triggered unintentionally by his current wife makes him stressful and worried, thinking that it may be happening all over again. Once his wife comes in the door he is very upset and he reacts strongly and disproportionately. His wife was late on account of some car trouble, she didn't call him because she didn't want to wake him. But will he believe her? Or perhaps he will but still suspect her a little. Once she senses this suspicion she will naturally be a little upset or sad having not understood why he should be suspicious in the first place. A problem was created out of nothing. Situations of this kind can very often happen between couples who have 'experience'.

Failed relationships make us less resilient to hardship, more emotional and more reactive, and usually cause us to give up more easily and more quickly the next time around. Most people, while recalling instances when they had arguments with their first or second partners, will realize that they were more patient and trusting then than they are now with their sixth or seventh one. It gets harder to trust men, for instance, when your first one or two cheated on you or were simply not honest with you. Moreover, the more we accumulate doubts, confusion and built-up cynicism from previous relationships about the subject of relationships, the less exciting and pure the subsequent one will be: things are always more exciting when we are relatively innocent and optimistic, when our heads are clear. They also reduce our general level of expectation of our newest partner and of the partnership we're trying to build; we are therefore no longer as romantic as we used to be – believing in dedication and devotion and that love is enough to conquer all. The cold fact of the matter is, when one no longer expects something, one most likely won't receive it.

Still, we keep trying in spite of everything, as we should. Until we don't. Relationships and love are so basic and fundamental to us all that we keep at it and don't quit easily; after all, it doesn't cost us money or involve too much hard work to meet new people and keep trying, so we do. But there are even limitations to that basic need and desire of ours, and after three, four or ten unsuccessful attempts we pretty much give up. Some people strike out on the second, third or fifth attempt and find someone more suitable for them, a better fit and have a relatively good relationship despite all the bad and failed ones they had in their respective pasts. But were two people to meet without having to go through failed relationships before, their current one would be even better and more successful.

The point I'm trying to make is that jumping from one relationship to another is not without consequence and severe side effects. I wish we would all realize this and therefore work harder at keeping our current relationships intact. We must realize as well that the other candidates out there are not necessarily better and easier to live with. Very often when we are young, we naturally feel that all our lives are ahead of us and that we will have plenty of opportunities to meet other great people. Believing this, when we run into more than the average trouble and difficulties in our current relationship, we don't try as hard to keep it going as we would have had had we been in our forties or even thirties. Breaking up our first or second relationship thinking that it would be easy to find someone else just as good, is often regretted by us years later after we have discovered that this wasn't true, and there aren't actually too many people out there with whom we can really connect, build and mutually fall in love.

I'm sad to see how many of us today have become more concerned with our own sense of economic security and with living a relatively comfortable life characterized by vacations with friends and the sporadic love affair, rather than a life of togetherness – a far cry from a culture or a world based on stable and productive relationships and family. No matter how many laws are passed in favour of individual freedoms and in favour of equal opportunities, or for economic and physical security, they will not make any person saner nor happier. They will merely reduce pressure and eliminate oppression and suppression. And even if many more will then have the time and money to engage in social betterment programmes and help others, no help or assistance is sufficient to undo one's loneliness, the lack of family and close ones; the people whom one can always lean on, trust and love.

Lately, the time period between relationships has become potentially as important and impactful as failed or broken-up relationships. The attitude embraced by many people when they divorce or break-up after a long relationship has become something of a phenomenon (it seems to me that, today, even three years constitutes a long relationship for many). A lot of women feel the need to be alone for a while, they just want to have some fun, to go on the occasional date and to feel free from responsibility and the sometimes-demanding life as a couple. Most say to themselves that it is temporary, they just need to 'live' for a while. Not really wanting nor capable of thinking long term they turn to these quick-thrills-no-commitment-fun-emotions, those we experience at the beginning of a relationship, when meeting a new person and when we have sex with a new person. Some only want to be by themselves for a while. Due to the reasoning and arguments laid out in this book none of these I believe is conducive or constructive and, as it turns out, it is very often during THAT time when many lose their way, their innocence or the ability to truly have and maintain the relationship they always wanted to have.

As with vigour and motivation, the ability to experience intense feelings and even simply to feel becomes eroded over time. The ability to feel love stems from the ability to feel relatively freely. This ability is very fragile; it quickly becomes impaired when we get hurt or disappointed. When we are innocent we are potentially able to experience our emotions in full. We can love fully and wholly. The more we get hurt, disappointed, the more we 'realize' that loving is no picnic and hence the less we believe in it. Consequently, we allow ourselves to feel love less; many of us also become afraid of falling in love. This often happens after a heartbreak, and with the next person we meet we try to 'go slow' and to tread cautiously; we are very wary of getting hurt again – we can even go so far as to say to ourselves, "I don't want to fall in love again", or, "I won't let myself fall in love again".

Without optimism and belief, one cannot experience one's emotions to the full. Non-belief or cynicism is the opposite of optimism; it's an anti-emotion quality. I'm still able to remember how I use to feel when I was young and in love. The intensity and the power of that emotion could and did sweep me off my feet. Today, unfortunately, occasions for feeling love and its related emotions and thrills are few and far between, and when they finally arise they are not as intense as they used to be.

Nonetheless, any person can still have a great relationship even if it's her/his third, fourth or fifth one. A person who's seriously looking for a serious relationship will still have the chance to realize it, even though the chances will somewhat decrease with each failed relationship; nevertheless, there is always a chance. People who think, though, that break-ups and failed relationships do not affect them and that they can jump from one relationship to another without consequence are mistaken.

The heart and mind have an expiry date – they almost never break down completely, but they can indeed become feeble, melancholic, pessimistic and cynical. Innocence and purity are synonyms. It is extremely difficult to remain innocent in the present day; nevertheless, you want to be as pure in heart and mind as you can for the right person when he/she comes along, giving yourself the best chance of realizing the relationship you envisaged in your most optimistic and hopeful moments.

At present, as we are becoming more and more introverted and individuated by technology, social media and virtual worlds, it is even more important to work out issues, to try to make things better in a family or a relationship, and to strengthen and better the 'togetherness'.

As long as we have faith and some zest left in us, there are things we can do to make relationships work, to make them fruitful and joyful.

Here they are:

Allow to be

I believe that the single most important thing in any relationship or interaction between people is to allow the other person to be him/herself and to support and strengthen that. To truly accept and embrace the way a person is, to support it and strengthen it. To positively allow a person to be is possibly one of the hardest things one can do, if not the hardest. Yet when it is done, it is the most rewarding thing for both parties.

The single most *calming* action that one can take or can be taken in any situation or interaction between people, or for that matter between any living thing, including animals and vegetation, is to fully let the living creature opposite you be!

Accept her/his dreams, goals; support them and try to help and encourage her/him to keep pursuing them. Fully respect her/his ideas and thought *processes*. Support what she/he does and the way she/he does it. That doesn't mean you shouldn't have your own opinions and that they cannot differ from your spouse's, nor that you should never voice your opinions. You should do, freely and openly, as well. You can do that and still be fully supportive and positively allow her/him to be. Imagine you're having a chat with someone you idolize or really respect, like someone famous. And in the midst of the conversation she/he insists on asking you for your opinion, which happens to be in complete contrast to hers/his. Picture the way you would convey your message and opinion to that person – I'm pretty sure it would be with the utmost respect, care, tact and affinity, and it wouldn't in any way be demeaning, devaluating or intrusive, right? Similarly, that is how you would approach matters with your spouse or anyone else whom you fully allow to be.

A prerequisite to having the ability to let the other truly be is to have the capacity to view the other as a unique person, who possesses her/his own mind, character, desires, wants, way of being, thinking and feeling: as a whole universe, and therefore to fully respect that person's sovereignty and not to judge her/him. Only then will it be possible for someone to fully let the other person be.

Having and exhibiting that capability or aptitude will support and strengthen your spouse and her/his life, and it will create a relaxed and calm atmosphere which will then allow your spouse to enjoy the relationship and life in general much more. This in turn will make everything easier, calmer and better for yourself.

This brings us to the second most important thing in any relationship, communication.

Communication

The second most important aspect of any relationship or interaction, whether it be with your child, boss or spouse, is communication!

Communication is the glue that holds all living forms together.

Communication is *agreed-upon* contact to one extent or another. When one doesn't want to listen or to have a conversation, nor to have any contact with another, even while the other is trying or reaching for it, this can hardly be categorized as communication

At the same time, when two people aren't speaking to one another but still live under the same roof, they are still in communication in a way: each of them is aware of the other's physical and mental presence and to one degree or another adapts his/her behaviour accordingly. But that will constitute a very low level of communication, indeed, borderline non-communication.

Communication requires an agreement on the part of the participants, whether it be minor or otherwise.

Nothing and nobody can live alone, unconnected to other forms of life or to other forms in nature – no flower, tree, lake, soil, bug, dolphin or human.

The symbiotic (which means 'living together') relations that all things share are based on communication; symbiosis essentially is communication. Such as when a particular strain of fungi living off of a plant's roots helps, in return, the plant to grow. Or the way the cells in our bodies get the mineral sulphur from the plants and animal products we consume. Plants and animals get it from the soil, which gets it from the ozone layer, which gets it from the algae in the sea. We are always in some way and to some degree communicating, whether it be directly, indirectly, silently or vocally.

When we're touching, listening, hearing, smelling, looking and obviously speaking, we're essentially communicating; interacting. When a flower emits its scent and we pick it up, we have just communicated with that flower. There was some contact between us, there was an exchange of something, energy, an idea. Even if we didn't reply, we accepted or agreed to receive the flower's communication, and that constitutes communication. Having done so, we now know more about that flower, it is less of a mystery to us, less of a stranger to us. The more we communicate, the closer we get to the people or things we communicate with and the more affinity we have for them and they for us.

One of the things that enrages us most is enforced silence. When this happens it creates a void in our understanding of the situation at hand and/or the person involved (why did it happen? Why isn't she/he saying anything?) Communication is required to fill that void – there's nothing we hate more than not understanding something. I suppose you can recall a time when you were given the silent treatment by a parent, friend or girl/boyfriend; I'm sure you hated it as much as I did. Due to the fact that everything in life is based on communication, people naturally and instinctively get upset and impatient when communication is cut short, distorted, twisted, or worse, when it's non-existent. When a person accumulates a lot of these communication break-ups or incomplete communication-cycles, he will basically have accumulated a lot of misunderstandings, almost like holes in one's knowledge and comprehension about someone, something or a situation. These will also contain some negative emotions: the upset, impatience or whichever negative emotions were present at the time the non-understanding occurred. Like, for instance, when one's partner gets upset or sad for no apparent reason but cannot or simply won't explain what had just happened or why it did. When that happens between two people often, you can be certain that their relationship will take a turn for the worse and suffer from a myriad problems. The couple in question will grow more and more apart, they will understand one another less and less, the feelings of frustration will grow and consequently their mutual feelings of affinity and love will subside and objectively they will no longer be able to call that relationship a good relationship.

More communication, not less, is always the better way to go about things. Indeed, sometimes you have to just step back, keep quiet for a while and let both parties calm down and regain their composure. But don't leave it for too long. Always resort to communication and attempt to reach an understanding. Don't leave matters unfinished, unexplained or unresolved, they will act like little mines in a minefield being built by your own four hands.

Sincere and honest communication can fairly quickly and amicably solve most problems in any interaction or relationship of any kind.

Good communication embraced as a basic tenet by any two people or a group of people will significantly improve the quality of their relationships and its chances of success.

We have established that open and honest communication is basic and extremely important, yet there are some things one should avoid uttering (especially men):

Don't ever tell a woman that you have doubts concerning her or the relationship nor that you're not sure if you love her. If you do have doubts, work it out quickly for yourself and make the right and fair decision for both of you.

On a lighter note, don't tell your wife or girlfriend that she might be a few pounds overweight or that her backside could be perhaps smaller or that her breasts could be little bigger. Women never forget, she may not mention that to you for years but it will stay in her mind, stuck, and it WILL shape the way she feels about you, trusts you and the manner in which she'll behave with and around you. And then one day, when you're not ready and you will have forgotten all about it, amidst an argument or during pillow talk, she will bring it up. Women, in general are far more sensitive to comments and criticism than men.

Owing to the demands the world has of women and the sometimes-burdensome public scrutiny placed on them; that of having to look good, be pretty all the time, as well as always being pursued and regarded as an object of desire; women more often than not take these expectations seriously and try to match up to them, and are therefore more responsive and sensitive to criticism.

More importantly, their outlooks on life and the importance they place on love, romanticism and the search for a lifelong serious relationship compel them to take matters and words more seriously and to heart – there is a lot more at stake or in the balance as far as women are concerned. Men don't usually look so far ahead in life and are not as romantic, thus things said to them don't shake their foundations so deeply!

Problems, difficulties and communication

Problems, difficulties, depression, upsets etc… more often than not, stem from the individual, from within, not because of the relationship or partner we are with. A large number of people believe that finding a partner will make some, if not all of their troubles, problems and difficulties disappear. That is almost never the case. Having a relationship can definitely make us feel better, give us more support, motivation and drive. Love can temporarily put us on a cloud and away from all the trouble. But it doesn't last; the feeling of love can, but problems and difficulties tend to reappear. Only when addressing the problem itself – a difficulty, depression and so on – can it then be truly handled and perhaps eradicated. That is not an easy thing to accomplish, but with an honest desire to change and by trying to work out ways to better oneself, perhaps also by getting therapy, one can improve one's disposition. A good way to handle or diminish personal difficulties is to remain active, keeping busy doing things that interest the individual. When you do do better you will find out an interesting thing – your partner will feel better too and the overall condition of your relationship will improve.

One sure way to get oneself to feel better and to improve one's disposition is to do good deeds and help others. It is very hard to conjure the will and energy to do much, let alone help others, while depressed, nevertheless it is indeed feasible. And if done, I believe it is the surest and quickest way for anyone to improve her/his mood and sense of wellbeing.

Yet, no one is perfect and living with someone is not a walk in the park. We all thus experience difficulties and the emergence and re-emergence of personal problems and hardship. When that happens, and emotions and perhaps irrationality take over, and you do happen to fight or argue with your spouse; try not to react, even when your partner is accusing you of something or is really upset with you. Don't worry too much about the way he/she is speaking or the tone of voice he/she is taking, try to remain calm and respond calmly. Most of the time you will defuse the situation that way, your partner will calm down and will *appreciate* your composure. This will contribute to you both by improving the level of your communication in general and also in enabling both of you to resolve matters more swiftly, more calmly and in a more respectful fashion in the future. Sooner rather than later you'll enjoy an overall reduction in the frequency and severity of outbursts and squabbles.

The difference between you responding angrily to your being calm and being on top of the situation is huge! We all know what happens when we start knocking each other. The argument then goes on longer and takes longer to get over. Staying calm can dissolve the situation very quickly (unless the angry party has real anger issues but even in that case going head to head with him/her, won't produce favourable results) and you both will feel better having solved it more maturely.

The next incredibly important thing we should avoid doing in a relationship comprises a big part of communication.

Lies

Be truthful, honest, do not lie!

I'm sure you've heard it before. But let's have a deeper look at the reasons why this is such a basic and vital aspect of relationships and life in general:

Lies are one of the worst offences a person can commit!

It is quite astonishing to see how a person being lied to by his loved one is more hurt and less forgiving than if the same loved one beat her/him, swore at her/him, didn't show affection and caring for a long while or even got drunk and kissed or made-out with another. Lying strikes at the core and fractures the very basic bond that exists between people. The crises lies can generate are more difficult to mend than almost anything else. Lies defy and shatter the fundamental value that holds societies and fuses people together: trust. Lies bring about distrust. Not much can truly exist in the absence of trust! It takes a long time to build trust and only a second to cripple it or destroy it all together. We are sensitive that way. Life seems sensitive that way when one takes the time and considers the fact that to build or create anything, whether it be a house, a new life, a painting, to grow a tree or flower or erect a bridge, it takes so long, an enormous amount of time when compared with the second or seconds needed to destroy that very same thing.

I strongly suggest that you don't lie to your loved one – nor to anyone else for that matter if you can help it. Also, keeping things from someone is in most instances exactly like lying!

When you make a mistake, come clean, confess right away. The longer you keep it to yourself the harder it will be for you to talk about it, the more it will metastasize within you and eventually distance you from the person you have been keeping that secret from – it's hard to look into somebody's eyes when you know you've lied to her/him, isn't it? After a while you start avoiding that person just so she/he won't make you uncomfortable; make you feel bad by constantly reminding you that you are keeping something from her/him

On the other hand, coming clean will earn you the trust of your partner and most of all will earn you the trust of you! The difference between one who accepts and confesses his/her mistakes to one who doesn't is huge. It is happiness, pride and success compared to introversion, discontentment, a degree of shame and smaller chances of succeeding in any relationship or endeavour in life.

Openness

It seems to me that now, more than before, women and men think that it is ok, or normal, to withhold information or things about themselves from their partners. "He/she doesn't have to know everything", "what he/she doesn't know doesn't hurt them", that kind of thing.

Not telling is similar to lying, with all its possible outcomes.

Openness is key in a relationship. The more open, frank and sincere a couple is, the better their relationship will be. This is of the utmost importance! One of the most powerful things two people can have between them is openness. When one opens up about one's emotions and thoughts, one feels better, closer to one's partner and his/her partner feels very much the same; it breeds trust and appreciation.

Many are ashamed of their past lives, deeds they have committed, things they do currently or people they meet. They may think that their partner might be jealous, won't understand or get upset. Some even fear that their partner will someday use that information against them. But when you commit to someone, as in marriage, you need to trust that person and vice versa. Any secret will fester and create infections, first in the psyche and then possibly even on a physical level.

Generally, women find it much easier than men to open up and speak about their feelings. In fact, most women love to talk about their feelings and emotions, a practice which is often met with some dismay or even irritation by men. In recent times men have indeed improved, and have become more open and capable of expressing themselves and their feelings, but the road to doing so regularly and freely is still a long one for most. Men! You can still be cool and express your feelings at the same time. It is possible!

The act of cheating

Very few things are worse than lying; cheating is one of them.

Cheating is a form of lying but it involves much more. When one is being cheated on, one is not only being lied to, one is also being conveyed a 'message' or impression that she/he is not enough, not good enough, that another is preferable to her/him. One's world is thus shaken and one's self-confidence and worth are reduced. Cheating is almost exclusively a reflection upon the cheater, and it reflects very poorly on him/her too. But it always makes the person cheated on self-conscious, introverted and also wonder whether something is wrong with them, whether they are good enough, whether it is their fault; not to mention the broken heart and the potential shattering of a person's plans and hopes for the future with her/his partner or as a family.

Even when one fully realizes that this behaviour stems from immaturity and insecurity and that it shouldn't reflect poorly on oneself, this realization is usually mostly on a theoretical level, so the act is always taken, to one degree or another, as an insult or personally. This shapes one's perception of things and life – and not in a positive way, either.

In addition, a person who's cheated on is put in a terrible position where she/he has to decide whether to give her/his partner another chance (if it is asked for) or break up. This is a very tough position to be in. If one gives her/his partner a second chance then she/he is then living through the coming months, years or perhaps forever with an uneasy feeling inside; distrust and a sense of broken self-integrity. It is hardly ever like in those movies when people can completely forgive and forget and move on with no serious repercussions.

If you decide to break up and preserve your integrity, rather than continue living with someone whom it will be difficult to fully trust again; when you take away the uneasy feeling and the broken integrity, you are left with all of the above and also alone; you lose your partner, husband/wife, the parent of your children.

The one who's done the cheating will suffer the consequences as well. He/she will never really be trusted again and that will most likely lead to other personal and social problems as well.

Betraying or cheating is a lose-lose situation for both. It creates ripples and has personal, familial and social repercussions in both the short and the long run.

Personal life

Another hugely important element that tips the scale for or against the success of an intimate relationship is how much of a personal life a person has. How much of a life he/she has outside the relationship. It is crucial to be yourself, respect yourself, pursue your dreams, have your own life, hobbies, goals. Don't centre your life around your spouse only, this is an unattractive and often repellent quality, one that only a possessive and jealous spouse would like (this type of relationship will have its own fair share of trouble and difficulties). The pivotal thing is being your own self.

Having a personal life, your spouse will possess the knowledge that you have a life outside the relationship and that it doesn't only revolve around him/her; you are neither only living for and feeding off of her/him, nor that he/she is all you have. When two people spend time apart it is refreshing and important but spending time apart pursuing your own interests, having your own personal life as well creates or keeps some distance not only on a physical level but also on a *psychological* level, and this is the truly significant thing. Having time apart pursuing your own interests means that some parts of your life are still separate and not completely dependent on your loved one and the relationship for their existence. Can you recall the way you were feeling at the beginning of a relationship, when you were not yet certain that she/he was fully yours, fully in-love with you or fully committed to you? Remember the little anxiety it created within you? We always want to be reassured or have it reaffirmed that the person we're with wants to be with us completely, that she/he is a hundred percent sure and decided about us. We also would like to have and be fully with the person we love, to have all of her/him. A similar feeling can exist at a smaller order of magnitude and be generated constantly when two people who are living together keep some of themselves to themselves. This leaves room for more, a space that will prevent your partner from being fully complacent and for taking the relationship completely for granted.

Being yourself and having your own life is a very attractive quality; it generates respect, which is hugely important, it invokes more appreciation from your spouse and therefore will make any relationship last longer and be better even when the fire and passion subside.

It is difficult to appreciate someone greatly when that person is needy and clingy and all that he/she has is the relationship and nothing else. This doesn't mean that a relationship can't work that way, but it will definitely be less enjoyable and likely last less long. Unfortunately, that is the rule in our universe: we desire the things that we can't have. Obviously, there needs to be balance to all of this: we can't play too hard to get, be too individualistic or be overly removed, that won't be productive. An intelligent perspective and experience will help to develop a very good and healthy balance which will enable you to love and respect each other for many, many years.

The important abilities mentioned in a previous chapter – letting the other be and the ability to be yourself – are to a degree built-in, encouraged or discouraged by the culture one lives in. Different cultures exhibit different levels of respect to the individual, his person and belongings. The more importance placed on respect for the individual in a culture, the easier it is for people from that culture to let the other person be, to give her/him space and the more naturally, indeed almost automatically, this psychological distance between people or a couple is attained. Again, here there is this balance: we can't give or show *too* much respect to our partner – that will make her/him almost a stranger. Nevertheless, making sure you're being your own self and having your own life will go a long way towards achieving respect, appreciation and likely more love from your partner, family and friends.

So, keep your hobbies, keep socializing, keep doing the things you did before you got married. Always look to enrich your life by learning something new or embarking on a new adventure or project. Work hard to make your own life full and interesting – I suspect that in that way and that way alone can you have a great and successful relationship with another.

All of the above does not mean or imply in any shape or form a lesser level of togetherness, of connection or closeness. On the contrary, having your own life will make the life you share with your spouse better, closer and warmer. Also, supporting one another will be easier. It is always easier to give support to someone or something when we feel contented in our own lives, when we lead a life which is pretty much full.

Women and men who have been in relationships for a long time, and feel they have not been true to themselves or have done enough of what they would have liked to, nor are they receiving enough respect or appreciation from their spouses, should not give up – it is never too late! Start now. Revive one of your interests or purposes, rearrange your life a little and go ahead and pursue it. It is never too late to study something, take dance lessons or learn how to play an instrument. A decision made at forty-five that it is too late to start something will be a remorseful and regretful one when looked at with hindsight ten years later. No matter how old we are, we are always us, our desires and passions do not change much and pursuing them will make us feel better at any time or age.

Little things are no small thing

Doing the 'little' things for our loved ones is exceptionally important.

Paying attention to the things she/he likes or doesn't like, to the way she/he likes to have things done or prepared, remembering important dates (especially if you're a man) and listening to her/him when she/he talks and remembering what was said; these, done in a sincere way mean that you respect the person you're with, as well as showing love (one of the definitions of love would be, 'thinking of' and 'caring for' someone). That will be deeply appreciated by her/him and will also make you feel good about yourself which, in turn, will strengthen the love you have for each other. Also, don't forget to say 'I love you' every now and then, women in particular need to hear that.

Don't be lazy or complacent when your spouse or children are concerned, I can't think of anything more important.

Do unto others…

Don't hurt your spouse – she/he is possibly the closest person to you and the one who will be there for you when no one else will. Be just, even when times are hard and life is beating you up from all directions. The ultimate test in life is doing the right thing by you, your spouse and everyone else around you that may be influenced by your decisions and actions. Each decision we make creates ripples which impact others around us and shape their lives as well. Each and every person is a whole universe with feelings, a heart and a soul. Try not to bend, degrade or demean any universe, any person. Always attempt to put yourself in the other person's shoes, envision you being him/her and then make an informed decision on how to react or how to go about the situation at hand.

Easier said than done? True. But you can start slowly, bit by bit. Begin with taking some time before reacting and before making decisions – that is fairly easy to do. After you've done that a few times, look back and assess those actions and decisions. Soon enough you'll find that you are doing better and you have changed.

I felt the worst when I hurt my parents, an ex-girlfriend or any other person for that matter. It is devastating to be broken up with, hard to get over and the memory of it stays with us and shapes the way we perceive relationships and the world. But when we hurt another it is an even *bigger* perspective changer as well as being hurtful to us.

Can you recall a time when you were about to break up a relationship and she/he started to cry? You must remember how hard it became for you to go through with it. More often than not we soften up and we give it another chance.

I once got jealous and very angry with a girlfriend of mine – foolishly, I might add. She was a beautiful person whom I had deep feelings for. Alas, back then I was a young male with a few of the traits that characterize many young males. One evening after she had inadvertently done something I didn't like, I angrily decided right there and then to break up the relationship. I drove her back to her parents' place which was an hour away; she was crying the whole way there. I cried too, but only after I had dropped her off and realized what I had just done. For months and perhaps a whole year after I regretted that I'd broken up with her. But for a much longer period, each and every time I recalled the way I broke up with her and how much I hurt her, I not only regretted it but felt awful and sad too. The latter affected me a lot more than the break-up itself.

Regret: "I shouldn't have done that", "I should have acted differently", "I could have", etc… We feel pity, ashamed, or simply dislike the way we acted, what we've done or said. When we accumulate a few of those we start to be disappointed with ourselves and our self-esteem is diminished. Lower self-esteem will reduce our chances of success in anything we set out to achieve in life. We'd better keep in mind that every time we do something regrettable in nature we are likely to fracture our own self-esteem a bit. We need all the self-belief and confidence we can conjure up for most of the things we try to achieve in life.

Political correctness

I'd like to say a word about free speech, which I prefer to call 'freedom of expression'. Freedom to express one's opinions, ideas and views is imperative for one's sanity and livelihood.

The fear of offending someone, a group or a minority – justified to a degree, has mostly been artificially injected into society by weak, ignorant and manipulative people. It has permeated the whole of society, crippling us to a marked degree and to the point where people are afraid to even express their tastes and preferences over a broad spectrum of matters and subjects. There is this shadow hanging over us like an unseen blanket of censorship, which we feel constantly even when we are alone: "someone could hear me", or "someone might be listening" – that kind of thing. This is chipping away at the sole true freedom humans have: freedom of expression.

Speak your mind, express your feelings and do not be ashamed or apprehensive about stating your taste and preference with regard to anything.

Tact is an important part of life, incorporate it into your ways and demeanour and all will be fine.

A tip for beginners

Owing to the reasons laid out in this book, many men don't think long-term these days and are looking to go out with as many girls as possible. They start a relationship, score, conquer the girl and then slowly distance themselves before leaving.

Women can reduce the effects and the length of these ordeals by exercising more prudence and trusting their intuition more.

Often, even at the very onset of a relationship, women can sense that something is not quite right, that the guy is not fully honest, is not being candid with her, namely on the subjects of marriage, family, children and settling down; he's basically not being serious enough. In the vast majority of cases the girl/woman, providing that she generally likes the guy, will choose to overlook these warning signs and see the better side of him, the good that may be in his eyes and heart. The problem is, most people do not live up to their true potential; life colours them with many extraneous layers of concepts, ideas and perspectives which become so thick that their inner selves cannot come out anymore, meaning that they are only *potentially* great. Women tend to see the good in people, which is a brilliant quality, but at the same time risky when it comes to relationships with men.

Not infrequently, I meet women at a stage of their relationship, a few months or a year in, dispirited and bewildered, the guy wants to break-up or showing obvious signs of no real desire to commit. They tell me how they thought the guy would change and how they had felt something was wrong from the beginning. I strongly believe in trying hard and giving people a chance, but at the same time as a woman you have to be vigilant. Don't waste your precious time waiting for someone to fundamentally change. Indeed, be serious, give the relationship all of its due attention. Still, in the early stages check and check again for his true intentions, make sure he's honest and that he wants to go the distance with you. People can change to a degree, and no fit is a hundred percent; we don't want to break up due to each and every fault or imperfection either of us might have. But when you sense or realize after careful, open, sincere and witty scrutiny (you don't have to lie or be secretive about finding out more about his intentions, it's your absolute right) that something substantial and fundamental is wrong, you'd better clear away, otherwise you're wasting your time, hurting yourself and inadvertently perpetuating this behaviour by men. Rare is the guy who suddenly after a few months realizes that he wants to be with you forever when at the start he was there only for the thrill of it or for a short run.

Aesthetic

Body

Although not directly related to our topic, I nevertheless believe that the subject of body aesthetics does merit some attention.

In a perfect world we should predominantly love others for whom they are and not place too much emphasis on looks. This perfect world might become a reality one day and it is something we should all definitely strive for. Alas, it is not here yet. In current society our bodies are our calling cards to an extent.

We generally seek to keep our possessions and things around us in a good and aesthetic condition; also, cleanliness is close to godliness. We like a clean, tidy and nice-smelling home to return to, a car to drive in, we love to enter a bed with brand-new sheets and fresh covers. We wash our clothes and dress nicely when we go out. It is important we do the same with our bodies. Our bodies, more than any other object or thing, should be tended to regularly and kept in the best shape possible. When one keeps it clean, smelling good and healthy one also feels better about oneself.

Being overweight, for instance, may be considered an unfashionable thing, undesired or un-aesthetic. But the thing that it really means more than anything else is that an overweight person is not in the best of health. This is simply unhealthy. Fat being accumulated in the body means that your metabolism in not working properly. Many other heath conditions can stem from this non-optimal one.

A word about nutrition: White flour products (normal bread {white}, pasta and rice to name a few) are as bad for you as sugar. This fact is unfortunately still not well-known.

Looks, appearance, the way one physically presents oneself comprise a part of the whole package a person brings with him/her to the table. Appearance is a feature, something that we take under consideration to one degree or another when we choose to be with someone. It is not as important as character traits, but is nevertheless important. Therefore, the way one presents oneself initially with regards to character and also appearance should be maintained. Just as one wouldn't like to see her/his partner behaving differently or exhibiting a different character after the two got married or having spent a long time together, the same applies with regard to looks and appearance. Many think that it is ok to let themselves go and not care too much about their appearance simply because they don't have to pursue or impress their partners anymore. Just because one's partner doesn't comment or make remarks about one's appearance of late and one's reduced self-sense of care, doesn't mean she/he is not feeling disappointed or even a little cheated.

An obsession with looks is definitely not a good thing. But a sense of aesthetics can keep things fresh on a physical level, which is indeed important.

Smell

I'd also like to take a moment and talk about odours and scents. Smell comprises a good part of our aesthetic makeup. The sense of smell is one of our main senses. Odours are an integral part of life.

In my opinion, some people don't pay enough attention to odour. Like cleaning up, dressing nicely, shaving and so on, body odour is, although not centre stage most of the time, a part of a person's appearance and her/his calling card nevertheless.

Our bodies emit foul odours at certain times and situations, which most of us try to combat, get rid of or hide. Smelling good is an attractive feature while smelling bad is a repellent one. When you smell good your partner loves to be near you, people like to be near you. The opposite is true when you don't.

There are different ways in which to go about keeping your body and clothes smelling nice. One of the ways that many employ on a regular basis is the use of fragrances. Speaking of which, I would recommend that everyone own at least two or three different fragrances or perfumes.

I've noticed that many people own only one perfume, one fragrance. They believe, and perhaps they are right in some cases, that their partner will come to know them by that one smell and as a result he/she will always equate that smell with them and be reminded of them, which is obviously supposed to be a positive thing. In my opinion it doesn't really work like that in most cases. We all grow tired of one particular fragrance eventually and a new one always makes us feel fresh and good all over again. I think it'd be better for women and men alike to own a minimum of two or three perfumes or colognes and to alternate between them every once in a while; that way things will remain fresh in the fragrance department.

Equally important is to not overdo it and use too much.

Making the body more pleasant and aesthetic is important and can really make a difference for the people nearest you.

Technology

I touched on this earlier, but I would like to expand on the subject. Technology can come between two people and deter or distract them from their actual lives together as a couple. Technology has its advantages but also detrimental effects: it drives us more inward, makes us more introverted.

Our attention today is mostly directed toward virtual stimuli. We pay less attention to the people next to us and more to the people we 'know' far away from us on a virtual network and to other addictive distractions like photos, videos and – worst of them all – scrolling down on pages or posts on phones or computers. The last one will surely diminish anyone's mental and psychological sense of wellbeing.

The addiction and indeed obsession with pictures, fast moving images, videos and posts basically means a desire to be or live a somewhat different reality or to live vicariously through something or someone else. They chip away at our ability to pay real attention to people and things around us and destroy our ability to focus. Any second we look down at our phones is a second we do not look up at the world around us and the people we live with. Any minute scrolling down pages on the net is a minute spent introverting and alienating oneself from society. We need to be on our phones and computers at times, of course, but very often we do it out of boredom and addiction. If we care to preserve our sense of wellbeing, we'd better be present as much as possible in mind, not only in body; looking straight up, looking around, observing people and things, making eye contact and being available for potential interactions.

When we look up, not into a screen or down at our phones, even though we're not involved in a conversation, meet and greet or some happenstance, we are then still available for all of these things to occur. We don't necessarily need them to happen every time we're outdoors and around people but only to be somewhat available for them to take place. That way, not only do we improve our own sense of wellbeing, but we are also making every place we go to more amicable, sympathetic and agreeable. Each one of us would prefer entering a place where people are looking up, making eye contact and not afraid to interact, as opposed to a place where most are looking down at their phones and basically saying that they are not really interested in any kind of interaction or that they are too busy at the minute.

Being or appearing available is the most basic ingredient required for having any semblance of a sane and properly functioning society. Yes, you can always come up to someone and strike up a conversation – we still do, and most people are happy to engage in one. But the chances these days for strangers to interact and the length and quality of these interactions, even between friends and close ones, are decreasing dramatically.

Imagine walking down the street and everyone you see and come across has their heads hanging down looking at the floor. How would you feel? wouldn't it be very strange, troubling and disheartening to you? If that was to become the norm could you still call it a society?

Society is moving in that direction, I'm sad to say. But we can change it and reverse the trend – I'm a serial optimist. We need only consider what we would like to have done unto us and then do the same unto others – we would of course prefer having strangers, friends and close ones giving us their full attention while we are speaking with them or while in their company. We would want them to be present and not to only be there physically with their minds and attention scattered or elsewhere. We would like that better, wouldn't we? Keeping all that constantly in mind, we can then devise the best possible ways to behave and be in company and society; combine our wants and desires while respecting others and giving them due attention. There has to be a balance in everything in life. But we do need to think, more than we currently do, about the people around us and more like people who live in a society.

I've come to greatly appreciate attentiveness and patience, traits that were fairly common up until the late 90s. I consider these qualities to be extremely important. I feel so good when a person really listens to me, when he/she is there in body and mind. That is true interaction, this is the only proper and honest way to interact and behave with people.

Unfortunately, the vast majority of us has already got used to people not giving us their full attention, being on the phone, etc… Getting used to something and not complaining about it does not mean that it isn't bothersome and upsetting anymore. Below the level of upset or anger and the impulse to react to things, exists apathy. It is a place we go to when we no longer believe something can change or get better. So, when you see or come across someone who still voices his frustrations about things, don't judge her/him too harshly and quickly – this person might be in a better condition than those who mostly keep quiet.

Have designated times, quality time for you and your spouse to spend together without the distractions of smart phones, computers or the like. Even sitting in the living room, separately reading books is a lot better than each being on his/her own phone or playing computer games.

These days, particularly when our lives are becoming increasingly dependent on technology, we have to make extra effort to share real quality time with our partners and children.

Try to have dinner together with no phones or any other distracting devices at the table. Go to the cinema, out to dinner or to meet some friends and leave your phones at home or turned off. When you are at home after dinner or you're simply spending the evening in, try to spend some time conversing with your spouse and/or children; real talk, with eye contact. Don't abandon yourself to endless virtual and electronic stimuli, they won't contribute to your relationship or life, and that is an understatement! (Scrolling down some posts, pages or videos and every once in a while sharing a funny video or post with your partner does not constitute a real conversation or quality time together.)

Laughter and Positivity

Laughter is a hugely appealing and attractive quality. We all love to laugh and we love people who make us laugh. Positivity is another major attribute which you should keep in mind when you're out there scouting for a mate.

When one possesses these two wonderful traits, positivity and the ability to make someone laugh, that person will win over the heart of any semi-intelligent person. These traits will make any relationship work better and remain fresh and interesting.

The ability to laugh depends on the listener's ability to find something to laugh about as much as it is on the joke-teller and the joke itself. The general, not momentary, ability to view things comically comes from within and it is pretty much in direct ratio to the person's level of contentment in life. The more contented the person is the more easily he can be made to laugh.

Women and old age

Cultures' perception of a man or his status stays pretty much the same even when he gets older, but it is very different with women. The advantages a woman has at a younger age turn into disadvantages when she gets older. Women are generally held in very high regard: they are considered and viewed as symbols of beauty, aesthetics and femininity. The gender to be desired, to be treated in a gentlemanly way and the gender that makes life interesting and challenging for men. Due to these, when they then get older and are not as attractive or beautiful, men's appreciation of them is substantially reduced. A woman's appreciation of herself thus lessens as well. Women are the ones who have the ability to give life, thus, the fact that older women are no longer able to bear children also contributes to their diminished appeal in men's eyes. Whether it be with older men who still haven't had a family and children or in general, men subconsciously always try to procreate.

Combine that reduction in appreciation towards older women with men's fear of death and their general insecurity and we can begin to understand society's current gloomy and unfortunate disposition – an older woman has a lot less appeal than a younger one.

Women are adamantly expected to be beautiful and feminine. That is why when men lose their looks it is considered much less of a big deal than when women do. And that is also why when men gain a little weight it is much less consequential than when the opposite sex does.

By and large this depreciation of women is sad and unfortunate and I'm sure all of us would like to see it change, and soon. We would all prefer to live in a society in which people desire to be with a partner or a friend because of her/his character and what that person brings to the relationship and not primarily because of her/his age or looks.

It's not fair to expect a woman to forever remain pretty and youthful. All of us age. Society should, through education, be focusing on substance rather than predominantly on looks and age. Things should largely go the other way around: the older one gets the more desirable one should become. A person, when older, especially a woman, is more mature, composed and has more knowledge of life. Women are also sexier when they are older – providing they still possess a fairly cheery attitude with regards to life, take care of themselves and are aesthetic. At the same time, we can understand and should not be overly critical with these general attitudes concerning women. After all, it is natural and normal to be a bit disappointed when you have great expectations and appreciation of something and that something changes. It's not unusual to want that thing to remain beautiful and desirable; in this case, women.

Still, substance, not age and looks, should be the dominant factor and until we get to the day when society has changed in that direction a woman can, if she so chooses, compensate for her age by doing some basic things like for instance keeping her hair long (if it used to be) - I find it really interesting that many women cut their her short when they get older. It is a bit of a mystery to me why they would do that. Indeed, thinning hair and loss of pigments make looking after it harder and some women don't like the way it looks either. But I'd like to offer more profound reasoning to why it is done. I believe that, as they get older, women sense (and are right to a large extent) that society no longer sees or regards them as young and beautiful. Very soon after, women reach the age in which they realize that they aren't able to have children anymore – which undermines their womanhood even further. Combined, these two factors push women to subconsciously and consciously submit and concede to society's 'verdict'. Going along with it, women then cut their hair short – the "society no longer views me as young, pretty and desirable, therefore I should no longer attempt to be" kind of attitude or thinking. It turns out they look even less feminine, womanly and appealing in my opinion, and without really realizing it, then justify or strengthen the 'opinion' society already had about them. This phenomenon has become much more prevalent in recent times. This is due to the increased focus and attention society pays towards looks and physicality. The more emphasis is placed on looks the more people are concerned about losing them.

To me, older women look great with long hair, they don't look ridiculous, they don't look like they are trying hard to be a teenager again. In my mind when a woman keeps her hair long it says to a degree that she still considers herself to be very much current and part of society and not on the fringes of it because she is already over the hill. It says to me that she still considers herself to be a feminine woman with all the related qualities. I know it is only hair but it does reflect a state of mind, perceptions and attitudes, so I believe women who still regard themselves to be pretty – much the same as they have been since their teens, through their twenties and thirties – possess very valuable dispositions to the female gender and to society in general.

Women! Don't feel too bad about getting older and give up to some extent or another on being attractive, pretty and aesthetic. Most of your charm comes from within and from the way you present yourself, which doesn't necessarily depend on how many lines and blemishes you have.

I understand how and what many women feel when they pass the thirty-years-old mark, when youth and looks start to fade a little. I say with empathy: it doesn't have to be a big deal. Know your strengths as a woman, believe in them and they will automatically be projected outward from within you and men will begin to view you as a young woman again. Believe in and understand your amazing power as a woman – femininity – and you can remain attractive and appealing for many years to come.

Being yourself, respecting yourself, pursuing your dreams and having as full a life as possible are all attractive, timeless and ageless qualities. Being true and honest to your feelings and intuition is the strongest you can be. Being so, will change – for the better – the way people in general perceive you and treat you.

One of the most important factors by far, which will sway the balance of people's opinions and views to one side or the other with regard to any person as well as contribute immensely to one's general success in life, is the level of one's internal happiness. The more cheerful your attitudes towards life are, the easier it will be for you to go about doing and achieving anything! Inner calm and contentment take ten to twenty years off a person's look.

"Be happy", is much easier said than done, but it is still possible. Try and better your inner and personal worlds by any constructive means possible. Knowledge, for instance (real objective knowledge, not usually the type you acquire in universities), equals good control; the more one knows the more control over life one has.

All that brings us to the time-frame within which women and men can do and achieve things in life:

Not all women care greatly about getting older, but when a woman does there are the things we talked about which she can do to make the process of getting older much less significant for herself and to stretch this period when she is changing from young and appealing to older and less appealing into a much longer period and with a smoother transition.

Still, some things do happen at different ages in life that there's not much we can do about. One of those renders women more vulnerable than men to the sands of time: that wonderful gift of the female gender, the ability to bring life, is over at around forty. Others are the eminently regarded qualities of women: femininity, attractiveness and looks. These, especially in the minds of men, generally take a hit around the ages of thirty-four to forty years old (to what degree? it depends also on the woman).

Hence, women have a shorter time span in which to achieve what they want to achieve with regard to relationships, love and family. Otherwise, these days, in other departments, a woman can reach her goals and targets in life just as well as a man can. Recently, in some parts of the western world, women have been able to achieve some things more quickly and more easily than men; the tables have partially turned. But if a woman considers love, relationships and family important I believe she should, for her sake, be more vigilant and responsible with her time and behaviour. Again, that's not fair and in a perfect universe it should not be any different to men, but it is what it is, especially from a biological point of view.

Dating Sites

Not many things are more destructive to our sense of belief, optimism and chances of success with regards to finding 'the one' and having a wonderful relationship than dating sites!

Soon after the inception of the internet, dating sites, or any virtual platform promoting dating for that matter, began to appear in abundance promising to provide us with a better shot at love and a big choice of people to choose from while flashing photos of some of their good-looking members on the front pages. Most of us thought it to be a good thing: a platform that would provide us with a big selection of people to choose 'the one' from, while also not having to go out so often and actively look for a mate – which can be really tiring and frustrating, especially when we get a little older, when we mostly prefer to stay in more than to go out.

We then join, sit back and spend hours going through photos and profiles, carefully choosing who to send a nice and personal message or a wink to. And then we wait, expecting a real response; an honest and simple communication like we usually have in real life on an almost daily basis. But dating sites are not real life. The replies we receive, especially as men, are far and few between, whereas for women they are often far from innocent or open and as trustworthy as they would hope for. Women in particular, very soon after they put their picture up often receive a handsome number of messages and after a couple of dates with the chosen ones pretty much realize what this platform is all about: not what they initially expected.

These platforms bring types of behaviour out of people that would otherwise be relatively concealed, controlled and not often acted upon. Men, being men, could not in the past openly and fully act upon their sexual urges and fetishes when society was free of internet and virtual pages to hide behind. A person in real life, in school, university, work or the pub is under scrutiny, he is there in person, seen and heard. He cannot get away with doing or talking about going out with two girls at a time, making advances to another and have his bizarre sexual desires fulfilled by yet another. Not without getting caught and suffering a blow to his reputation. Nor could he try to score with as many women as possible without repercussions – unless he makes sure he dates women from different cities or areas, something much more complicated to achieve before the internet. A person's natural habitat is relatively small and the people in it are pretty much connected to each other in one way or another. Eventually one of the girls he's fooling around with will hear about another and his mischief and the saga will pretty much be over – and so too his good reputation (mainly with the ladies, that is). Furthermore, most of us feel some shame and self-consciousness when we do things we know are not ok. It is easier for us to do these when no one can see or know about them, when no one is there to rub it in our faces – we feel embarrassed knowing that people know. Which is why when one can remain relatively anonymous one can allow oneself to say and do things that one wouldn't otherwise say or do when in the company of people that may know or recognize one. And what better place to hide and act upon one's unethical and immoral urges and behaviour than on dating sites? Especially these days when sex has become so central to people's lives.

Therefore, on dating sites women have a really tough time finding someone who's truly serious and honest. They very quickly grow wise to this reality and become less and less trusting of men, which in turn makes it even harder for them to find someone.

To compound the problem, good-looking women get between five to fifty or more messages daily. How can anyone compute and choose properly scrolling through an average of ten or twenty messages and faces a day? With how many men can a woman have a proper conversation with over a virtual page? How soon will it be before one guy looks and sounds just like the other? Faces become pretty much soulless photos after a very short while. How much of a chance would a woman have to really suss out a man who writes to her or to see if there is chemistry between them? How much can one know about another communicating this way? One sentence spoken face to face is worth fifty written as messages on a dating site! This makes it really hard for women to choose wisely whom to give a chance and meet with.

Another way in which dating sites act destructively is by giving us the impression and the illusion that there is a big and endless choice of people to choose from out there. What it does is plant this seemingly true datum that there are always other people we can meet and they are available on those sites. Therefore, 'armed' with this knowledge, we very often, while on a date with someone or in the early stages of a relationship, allow ourselves to be quite petty and critical. We don't truly give people enough time to show their true colours nor do we pay enough attention to what might be their positive sides or give it time to develop into something. We feel that we can always go back to the website and find another person, possibly a better one; after all, we're looking for the best one for us. It turns out we often give up at the first sight of imperfection or the smallest appearance of something we don't really like or agree with. This belief that we can always go back to the site and find someone better and more suitable for us is impairing our ability to fully be with the person at hand, find out more about this person, discover good things about him/her and to perhaps make something out of this relationship.

Each one of us is a whole universe with a unique character and things to offer. By being on these sites we are reducing ourselves to the level of a mere photo, an almost non-spirit, empty vessels. How can a human being, even when she/he is considerate, thoughtful and objective remain so when she/he is faced with hundreds upon hundreds of small photos of people's faces crammed together lifelessly on a few pages? Have you ever looked at a photo of someone and said, oh, she/he is ok looking, not bad, and that was it, but then saw her/him in real life, talking, moving, smiling and all of a sudden felt that she/he was appealing, cute, attractive? I know I have, quite a few times.

Dating sites make us out to be predominately virtual figures; lifeless and emotionless.

Still, there are successes, some do meet on dating sites, have relationships and even get married. But how many? Check it out for yourself objectively. The numbers are much lower than you would expect. And with all that big choice. Moreover, many who do meet through the internet are often a little more 'damaged' than the people who have never used the internet for dating. This makes it harder for them to develop and maintain a successful relationship.

The damages dating sites cause are far greater to society than the alleged benefits. The huge amplification of the distrust in men women already possess is the biggest and most harmful drawback of that system. I've spoken with and met numerous women who've been on dating sites: their distrust of men was overwhelming! They 'knew' that men are not to be trusted, they 'knew' that all men want is to have sex, they 'knew' that all men are liars!

With regard to men, they, in general, keep getting worse. It seems like more men these days are trying to live lives of no consequence. (I'm sad to admit that I used to be a bit like that until a decade ago). And while they come in contact with women who understandably have doubts and apprehensions about them, upon realizing that, they are then further pushed down this road they are already on. "They don't trust us anymore nor do they expect us to behave any differently, so we may as well keep doing what we've been doing". In other words, the inability to resolve the problem is perpetuating the problem and that perpetuation is further increasing the problem; making more and more men jump on the wagon and behave badly causing more and more women to distrust them even more. It is like thick mud that we've all walked into and it is getting soggier and soggier by the day.

You need not do or say much in order to persuade a person today that men or people in general cannot be trusted. When one has experienced distrust at first-hand on a number of occasions, one will become sensitive and cynical at the first sign of anything that might suggest disloyalty, infidelity or lying. She/he will quickly suspect and doubt the deed or the thing being said.

Important note: women are not all saints and a growing number are using dating sites or other sites to pursue sexual adventures and nothing more. At the same time there is a large number of men who are looking for a serious relationship and who can also be trusted.

Being curious in nature, I asked quite a few women how many men they managed to meet or date during the time they had spent searching for 'the one' on dating sites. Women who spent months upon months on sites went out with no more than between five to a dozen of guys and the vast majority of them have not yet found 'the one'.

Anyone can meet more than five or ten people she/he could perhaps go out with during a period of several months – providing the person is open and willing to meet people. This can be done simply by going out once or twice a week to cafés, live concerts, dance classes and the like. In addition, dates arranged by two people after having met face to face by chance or by an introduction through a friend would be, most of the time, much more productive and honest than a date arranged on a dating site. We can learn much more about a person meeting him/her face to face or being around him/her than when 'talking' with him/her on a virtual page. The decision then to give it a chance and date that person is much easier to make after having observed him/her for a few minutes or longer in a café, at a party or a dance class.

We're fooling ourselves thinking it is easier to find someone on dating sites where we believe there is a bigger choice, (indeed there are more people there to choose from but it is not a real advantage when the level of seriousness of many is so low). In actuality we can meet more people in real life just doing the normal things we use to do and perhaps by adding another group activity once or twice a week. And, more importantly, staying away from dating sites will preserve the little trust we all still have in others – or at least won't ruin it as quickly. That means we will still be able to maintain a little belief and innocence. This in turn will delay or even stop us from rendering ourselves too cynical to be able to begin or have a successful relationship or even from maybe giving up on the whole thing.

Women, I recommend that you stay out of dating sites. If you do succumb to pressure or the need and urgency to find someone, don't spend more than a month or two there. Give it a chance but take it very seriously, vet the guys as well as you can, meet one or two and take it from there. If you haven't succeeded by then, keep in mind that generally the longer you try the smaller your chances to succeed will become.

Not only women woe that reality. The way some men behave, the large number of messages men send and the dishonesty a lot of them exhibit make it harder than it already is for men who are serious and honest to find a serious relationship on dating sites.

There are many things you can do to meet honest people, people who are not necessarily hiding behind virtual pages and under false pretences. Be more patient. Resist the appearance of abundance and the seemingly large choice of good-looking and cute men.

Alarming trend

Recently, as the trend to becoming less feminine and the emasculation of men is spreading another trend has emerged; the push to completely obscure the lines between the genders. This is being embraced by a small but slowly growing number of people in various parts of the western world. It is one thing to let people choose whatever or whoever they want to be but when universities and governments create or legislate educational policies to support, enhance and expand that trend followed by big chain stores and corporations going along and promoting the same thing, then we are faced with a big problem. The cessation of the production of gender-based toys by a few big chain stores is but one example of the direction these people are following or taking, ignorantly or otherwise. Making women more masculine and tougher and men play with dolls will not serve us in any way, shape or form as a society; on the contrary, the repercussions could be devastating. Three to five thousand years of recorded history backed by eons upon eons of well-known and agreed-upon axioms in biology and chemistry are being swept aside and disregarded by people who think they know better. Indeed, we can have women 'man up', work on their muscles and even become infantry soldiers – to what end though? Just so we can say that people are equal (more like the same) in every way now? We can never bridge the biological and physical gaps between men and women. And even if we could, do we really want that? For what purpose? Isn't it a better and more beautiful world where two DIFFERENT genders exist? Two genders that complete one another. Isn't the world a much more affable and pleasant place with feminine, graceful and classy women in it? A world without femininity is like a beautiful oil painting that has lost its colours. One of the more graceful and truly beautiful human features is femininity. That ridiculous idea that women can and should be like men is horrific. What's next? Men giving birth? Were these ideas to take hold among bigger sections of society we could be facing a reshaping of our civilization within a generation, which will be disastrous. I believe I can speak or write intelligently on the reasons why some people would go down this road but all I care to say at the moment is that I feel that these people, their ideas and agenda are all very dangerous to us all and to the future of our society.

Marrying young

Every so often I meet a young woman who is really eager to get married. She would really like to be somebody's Mrs. She loves the concept of marriage. She is anxious to be a wife.

The idea of marrying young used to be standard up until seven or eight decades ago. Even as little as thirty years ago in the western world and up until a decade ago in some cultures many would still marry fairly young. But now this concept is being demeaned and degraded in its entirety to a large extent. It is not considered 'cool' anymore to want to marry young. It is thought by many to be unintelligent and silly. This is a pity.

A few months back a friend of mine told me that when she looks back on her last relationship she realizes that she was a different person then and that today she is more mature, sees things differently and that she's not sure whether she would go through that experience and be with that boyfriend again if she were given the opportunity to do so today.

That is how she feels, and this is true to her. But as an objective observer I wish to point a potential problem with that statement: we are constantly changing! Five years from now we will be a little or a lot different, we will see things differently and have a different outlook on life. When you get to a stage where you feel very mature, five years from that point you'll feel more mature and you will look back at the previous time when you thought you were mature and say, 'and I thought I knew life then!'. This is true for most people. We keep changing simply because we are moving forward through time and experiencing life more. Things never stay the same. Indeed, our perspectives change at different degrees and at varying rates. We change at certain ages more than at other times, at different stages more than at others and after particular events or sets of circumstances. But change, whether it be big or small, is continuous.

Taking all that into account, when then should one commit to another and get married? The most sensible answer would be when we turn sixty-five years old, right? Makes sense – by then we will pretty much be the most mature and experienced that we can be and thus we could make the best and wisest decisions and have the best possible relationship. Well, I'm sure we wouldn't want to wait that long would we? And we couldn't. First, we all have, especially women, a biological clock. Second, we don't live forever or even to a hundred and fifty.

So, if we keep changing and we will never be at the best shape of our lives at one particular point, maturity- and experience-wise, then it doesn't really matter, we can marry at any age. Maybe at thirteen? Well, that might be too early. So, which is the correct answer? What is the right age? Who can tell us when the best time for us to get married is? The answer is, only us. Individually, each should choose on his own according to her/his desires, level of readiness and the level of her/his self-confidence regarding the future success of the marriage. It can be at any age that is practical. Some can be mature enough and have their lives planned and set on a course by the age of eighteen. Some need to be older.

Some believe that the changes they go through between the ages of twenty and twenty-five are bigger and more significant than later in life. This is the case only for some. Many go through bigger changes between the ages of twenty-five and thirty and others at different ages yet again. The point that I'm trying to make is that people feel the desire and the readiness to be married at different ages and stages in their lives and we as a society should not condemn or condone one specific attitude or the other.

There is a very strong argument for marrying early and in favour of the young ladies who would like to do so. When you marry early you avoid the time-consuming and often arduous process of dating and searching for 'the one'. A process which these days takes longer and longer for more and more people and one which can produce no little heartbreak and disappointment. Second, when you marry early you set out to achieve what you set out to achieve as an individual with less distractions, with more focused attention and with much more help and support. Living together and supporting one another makes life more relaxed and easier. This is a huge plus for anyone to have. Even if one would like to travel a little, see the world or maybe embark on different adventures or attend different schools it does not mean one cannot do so and keep a relationship at the same time. When people love one another and are decided on their futures together no six-month trip or a period of a couple of years seeing one another every other weekend will wreck that bond.

Perhaps the young lady who is anxious to get married is drawing her motivation and the image of married life from movies, her parents' education or the example they have given, ideals or fairy tales. Does it make it less real for her? Does it make it less valid? Does it make it less possible? No. There are plenty of people out there who grew up believing and desiring the same scenario. If cultures were to validate, support and respect any type of thinking and attitude more will be free and allow themselves to think and plan like these young ladies and more will succeed in realizing their goals in relation to marriage. Instead of perhaps waiting, living together for a few years and then breaking up, like many do. When you don't commit, you don't commit. No matter how well you think you're going and how much you believe you love each other, fights, disagreements, outside pressure or any other little thing can fracture the bond between you more quickly and easily than if you were both much more committed to one another, i.e. married. Any relationship would be more stable and have a better chance of success this way. How much better? I believe, overall, at least twenty percent less would get divorced. It's not for nothing that women very often seek the man's commitment.

So, we got married, each in her/his own time, what happens when we change, then? When we have more experience? When we grow more mature? How do we bridge the gaps in points of view and attitudes between us if and when they appear? We work it out! We simply go through the changes together, making an effort to accept, *understand* and respect the changes each of us go through and try and work out ways to somewhat bridge those gaps and make it possible to still live together and cooperate as a couple. 'Understanding', real understanding is probably the biggest bridger-of-gaps we have in our tool box. One should first understand oneself; that way one could more easily deliver one's point of view, thereby having a better chance of making the other side understand and very possibly of accepting as well. When the decision to be and remain together is firm and rarely doubted, two people, together, should and can overcome many an obstacle.

And if we grow apart to the extent where it is impossible to share a life anymore, we break up, get a divorce. But, there is a lot to be done and many ways to go about working things out before letting it all go. It is all down to the viewpoint one takes; when one perceives marriage to mean a strong bond for life and a very important one too, then one is willing to go through a lot to keep it going and learn to accept the differences between her/his spouse and oneself. This does not mean compromising to the degree where one loses her/his integrity or to the extent where one feels really hurt or unhappy in the relationship.

I've been noticing an interesting phenomenon between couples that I believe deserves consideration. There appear to be fluctuations in the degrees of affection and closeness two people in a relationship feel for one another. I do not refer to the daily possible changes in moods and disposition but to the more general and long-lasting ones that occur every few months, a year or longer interval.

Obviously, emotions are strong at the beginning but after a year, two or four there will often be a dip in the level of affection and sense of closeness. Then after a while there will very often be a resurgence of these emotions. This time though these emotions of closeness and love feel a little different from the ones the couple had in the beginning. Then, a year, two or three later there could be another slump and then a surge again, and again things would feel different this time around. That 'different' is not a negative thing, it can often be a positive 'different'. Due to the passing of time and going through the ebbs and flows of the relationship, the couple get to know each other better, they get used to one another more and last, but definitely not the least, the bond between them becomes stronger. Which is mainly why when there is a surge and things are good again it might even feel better than before.

However, people usually feel a bit lost during those dipping periods and are a little less sure about their relationship and therefore also more susceptible to outside influences and stimuli. But when the dip is over and the couple's mutual emotions are high again the certainty in their relationship is back and they are focused on their relationship once more and are in turn much less susceptible to exterior influences. We'd better take that into account if and when things are not going great between us or when we feel that our emotions for our spouses are not as strong as they used to be. Things can go back to being on the up and up again and even better than before. I've seen it happen with *plenty* of couples.

The alternative or 'easy' way out which many take today is to break up or get a divorce. Recently this has become a trend, breaking-up, separating – quite an appealing proposition for many who seem eager to be free, whatever that means today. They think that being alone is being free. In this day and age to be left alone, to answer to no one, to have or take less responsibility, to go out with different partners and to experience sex with new people is considered freedom. Some though honestly believe that they might find someone better or a better relationship. Alas, when people divorce in their fifties, the chances they will start something new and better are not very high. Most end up living alone, not wanting to commit to anyone anymore. Today, for many people relationships mean too much work.

For men the situation is much worse. Woman, unmarried can still manage, they are ok being alone. When men, who are normally unable to stay or live alone, get divorced, thinking there is a big pool of women to choose from out there, more often than not end up alone and not in great shape either.

It is quite sad to see anyone alone without companionship, without someone who cares for him/her and someone to care for, no matter whether young or old, but particularly when at an advanced age.

Have a look at your parents, grandparents, their parents – there are many bad and sexist stories, but there are good ones as well. Ones that show two people going through a lot and coming out the other side stronger and more bonded. At least in a much better condition than they would have been had they divorced and had gone their separate ways. The point here is not to completely and utterly compromise nor to capitulate and lose your integrity, dignity and self-respect, but to view the institution of marriage more seriously and to work harder at keeping it intact. The rewards for hard work and making things go right once again are numerous and very gratifying.

Closing words

Time is moving forward, things are constantly changing. We live through time hence we live through 'change'.

Necessity is another thing which drives us towards 'change' and changing.

Our bodies and biology are based on 'change'. Nothing can live without 'change'.

Therefore, we all expect 'change' to occur. Whether it be in us, in the people we know, work or in society and the world. Because 'change' is so basic many of us have even become fond of it, fond of 'change' or changing. Some have become so infatuated with 'change' they relish it; they keep making changes in life and to things. We can see it everywhere – I'm sure you know one or two people who constantly bring up new inventions, talk about new developments in technology, relishing in the changes that are taking place. Often, many of us feel a degree of joy or even pride from talking about the changes our country or society have been through.

When the obvious and expected process of 'change' is combined with the absolute belief of people that each new generation is somehow better and more advanced than the one before (partially based on facts but still mostly a belief) plus the much-admired concepts of 'new' and 'advanced' talked about earlier, we get a force that is constantly trying to push forward. Well, how is all of that related to our subject?

Due to that constant push ahead, among other important reasons mentioned throughout this book, an increasing number of individuals today view and consider the old-fashioned ways of the past, the grace and class of the feminine women of yesteryear and the gentlemanliness of decades and centuries past as old and irrelevant. They are intrigued by new concepts, ideas and philosophies that don't necessarily make any more sense or are logical, but because they were conditioned to think so. Obviously, many things need change and improvement, but many do not, especially basic concepts which concern people's welfare and sense of wellbeing, such as the quality of their relationships and interactions – these are everything in a society, and thus in life.

The trouble with the easiness with which people accept or embrace change is that many ill-intentioned or ignorant people prey on that and exploit it. As opposed to many good and ordinary folks – numerous groups, some reporters and others like some politicians who work hard and invest time and effort in order to bring about good and substantial changes like those needed in countries run by dictators and to cultures which still exhibit flagrant inequalities and injustices or simply for the betterment of our quality of life and security – some people are obsessed with *constant* social and cultural changes regardless of whether they are truly needed or what the consequences are. These individuals, either advancing someone's agenda, trying to create new, financially viable markets or simply to generate 'change', usually end up working for media outlets: on TV, in the film and music industries, on radio stations and on the internet – after all, the media always try to provide us with something new, fresh, 'cool' and interesting, they thrive on 'change'. Thus, in spite of the fact that the number of people whose faces and voices we've come to know, those working in media, is relatively small and that most of us, deep down, would like to keep the status quo on most things – not have them change so quickly or at all – we find ourselves, mainly young people, being bombarded and brainwashed on a daily basis by new concepts and ideas that are slowly but surely infiltrating our individual and collective consciousness. Quite a few of these are major and life-changing. Many people have their minds changed with little resistance, and this includes some politicians and university professors.

Concepts like: don't cheat, don't do drugs, have a stable family, don't be promiscuous, women should be feminine and have grace and class, these used to be elementally accepted and intrinsic in the past and much more adhered to compared with the last fifty years – definitely when compared with the last decade. The push by the individuals mentioned has brought many today to show enormous flexibility with regards to these concepts: the horrible practice of cheating has been almost legitimized in the western world; being promiscuous is not such a big deal anymore; the opposing idea to a stable marriage – 'monogamy is no longer possible' – is prevalent today; the silly and ignorant belief that drugs are not that bad has been gaining support from all quarters; and the one about 'equality' – which drives women to think that they should be like men, to name a few. Finally, the institution of marriage as a whole used to mean much more to people up until three generations ago and not only concerning fidelity.

If we as individuals and as a society won't stand up for our personal convictions and keep our integrity intact, instead following the subjective, short-sighted views and imprudent policies of particular individuals or groups in positions of power or influence, we will end up living in realities and societies we really dislike, to put it very mildly. Standing up for what we believe has never been simple, unfortunately. It is very much like swimming against a strong current: it's tiring and in most cases the current prevails. Still, at times, we prevail and we also save the person next to us and they in turn save another. We'd best listen to our inner selves and consciences, be the best we can be and lead by example. That way our immediate environment and then the town, city and country will see a change fairly rapidly.

I believe we have no more than a decade to turn things around. Beyond that point it will be very difficult, possibly impossible, to reverse. Young people today more than ever need good role models: men and women with backbone and substance.

Women! You are the chosen people. Chosen to be feminine: graceful, aesthetic, classy, beautiful and to give life.

Femininity is one of the greatest gifts, cherish and revel in it.

Femininity is the human manifestation of art, *you are all artists in a way.*

Men! Women respond very favourably to men who understand them. Try to understand her history and biology and she won't seem so complex anymore. Also, be honest, put your money where your mouth is. Be respectful and be a gentleman. Stay strong and virtuous; it will keep the demons at bay.

We would all be much better off living in a world filled with Femininity, with grace, class, ladies and men who are truly gentlemen. We would benefit greatly from having more graceful women walking around and more gentlemanliness to accommodate them. Nothing here goes against or contradicts equal rights and opportunities. Society can be based on the family unit with distinct and beautiful differences between the genders and still be advanced and move forward in many other areas of life. Love, respect, fidelity, truth, honesty and the family unit are the pillars on which any society rests at any given time or place.

I'm of the opinion that when a woman accepts her femininity she'll gladly accept gentlemanliness. Women can go back to the understanding that being treated in a gentlemanly way is a good thing: respectful and power-giving to women and not the other way around. Being rough and tough like the classic man will not necessarily get a woman further in life, but grace and class will for sure.

Today, more than ever, is the time to be feminine. There are laws against harassment, men are pretty much obliged to respect women and women have equal rights and opportunities in many countries. Women can concentrate on aesthetics and grace if they choose to – I'm fairly certain that this will be warmly welcomed by most.

In relation to sex, let's not cheapen it to the degree where it becomes mechanical. By that point we most likely won't be able to really enjoy it anymore. By then it will have become more a satisfaction of a need than real pleasure. Sex without intimacy is cheap. Intimacy normally requires time and chemistry on a *mental* level.

With regard to our physicality – looks fade! A general inclination for aesthetics as a character trait as opposed to simply being good-looking is much more important and productive in the long run. Besides, ask yourself, how long do you think it will take for you to stop looking at her/his pretty face and begin to notice his quirks, idiosyncrasies and behavioural patterns? We marry and live with a *person* and this means many things or aspects, a lot more than only her/his outer shell.

And let's not forget differences. We should cherish and relish them. Absolutely nothing will work in this universe without differences. If things were the same they would cancel each other out. Differences make life possible and interesting. We don't need to look at changing basic natural laws in order to make life more 'interesting'. Life can remain interesting enough the way life is for many millennia to come. With regard to the differences between women and men, they are absolutely necessary if we would like to still be attractive, interesting, appealing and intriguing, and have chemistry with the opposite sex. Chemistry, whether between chemical elements or people is only possible when differences exist. 'Chemistry' is the unique, cheerful, exciting and often thrilling joining or potential juncture between two different things or people.

Which brings us to:

When a couple is joined together a relationship is created and another world is formed. Each of us has her/his own inner world; a rich world filled with one's own character, experiences, memories, wants, desires, passions – all of which uniquely comprise a person. Joined together, two distinctive and intriguing worlds create an additional world, a shared one which is distinctive and potentially intriguing in its own right. When created upon mutual love and respect, such a world will enrich the individual worlds of the two involved. The closer the two individuals' worlds get and the longer they are joined together, the bigger and fuller their joint world will be. The more love and respect given while building a joint world the lovelier and more rewarding this new world will be.

One thing is very important to remember when building a joint world and that is 'compromise'. Compromise is not a bad thing: on the contrary, when you do compromise (to a degree of course) and your partner fully appreciates and acknowledges it then the feeling of 'compromise' transforms into something else, something with more positives than negatives in it, unlike what the word compromise might suggest.

Generally, when we do things for others and they are received with appreciation and acknowledgment it makes us feel appreciated; good about having done the deed and also about ourselves. The appreciation from others is even bigger when we, *without* dissent or resentment, compromise; do things for others which we don't necessarily want to or feel like doing. Acting thus will often make us better people fairly quickly! Receiving appreciation and feeling good will 'soften' us and therefore enable and encourage us to give even more to our loved ones as well as to other people. This process will teach us more about ourselves and our abilities; it will show us that it is possible for us to be even more understanding towards others than we initially thought – less rigid or set in our ways. It will demonstrate to us that compromising can make others feel better and at the end of the day, 'compromise' is not that bad. As a result, we will be able to accept others more; when one can bend or adjust – compromise – one can then accept more different behaviours, attitudes and types of character. Thus, as long as love, respect and appreciation exist, 'compromise' could in actuality mean a good and positive thing for us.

Optimism: We can't simply turn the optimism switch on and off. Still, we really need to try and regain it each time we lose a little of it. In my opinion, possibly the only way to remain mentally and physically healthy for life is to stay optimistic.

Expression: When one keeps things inside one hurts oneself. And as a result, less truth and honesty will see the light of day. We owe it to ourselves and society at large to voice our opinions even if they go against the norm or the grain.

And finally, "Ladies and gentlemen" is one of the most common and classic salutations. Let's again give these words and the order in which they are said the meaning they deserve and used to have!

I hope your journey with me through this book has been a pleasurable one, one that may have reaffirmed what you've already known but couldn't or never really had the chance to utter or articulate. A journey which has inspired you, even if just a little, to a better life for yourself and the people around you.

ABOUT THE AUTHOR

Ayal was born and raised in Israel. He has been a musician since an early age and a therapist for the last sixteen years. He currently resides in Poland.

ACKNOWLEDGMENTS

I would like to thank my parents for their continuous and loving support, without which this book might have not been written.

I'd also like to thank my sisters for their love and encouragement, my cousin David Nekava for his help with choosing the title for this book and Jonathan Stapleton for proofreading and editorial input.